C000107859

STUFF AND NONSENSE

Stuff and Nonsense

Observations
of a Norfolk Scot

Logie Bruce Lockhart

Line drawings by the author

Larks Press

Published by The Larks Press
Ordnance Farmhouse, Guist Bottom, Dereham
Norfolk NR20 5PF

01328 829207

Printed by the Lanceni Press, Fakenham, Norfolk.

March 1996

This book is dedicated to my wife and family
who made it such fun.

ACKNOWLEDGEMENTS

*Thank you to the following newspapers and magazines for their kind
permission to reprint articles which first appeared in their pages:
The Eastern Daily Press, The Spectator, The Times Educational Supplement,
The Times, The Field, Country Life, The Lady, Woman, The Dalesman,
The Daily Telegraph, The Guardian, Choice, She, Sports Teacher.*

British Library Cataloguing-in-Publication Data
A catalogue record for this book is available from the British Library

Copyright: Logie Bruce Lockhart, 1996

ISBN 0 948400 40 4

CONTENTS

Youth - *p. 1*

Family Life - *p. 19*

Fun and Games - *p. 35*

Norfolk Life - *p. 53*

Education 1 - *p. 69*

Education 2 - *p. 95*

Why 'Stuff and Nonsense'?

Some flattering E.D.P. readers have from time to time encouraged me to get some of my articles since 1960 published in book form. My publisher was bold enough to advise me to entitle the motley collection 'The Wit and Wisdom of Logie Bruce Lockhart'. Although I am tolerably conceited, this was too much for me, and much too much for my wife, who, like all good Headmaster's wives has deflationary gifts. 'Stuff and nonsense!' she said.

This rang a bell; how appropriate! These reflections contain a lot of tongue in the cheek nonsense, but also some 'stuff': family life, education, games, fishing, natural history, art, music, childhood, old age, life and death at which we can either laugh or cry. Where possible I have tried to prefer praise to condemnation, laughter to tears, although after 27 years as a Headmaster, I have not always avoided the pomposity characteristic of my trade.

Extraordinary luck has come my way. I had a privileged and blissfully happy childhood, although never wealthy, which is a hopeless start for a writer. By tradition, scribes should have an unhappy childhood and be bitter ever afterwards. Some shocks in war time, a sight of Belsen and the loss of a beloved child, however, made me very conscious of the thin ice on which even the most fortunate skate.

I was especially lucky in my parents, my wife, whom I found in a train, and my family, and in the rare gift of a career which I enjoyed. My father had a wide range of interests from painting and music to French literature and games; in trying to imitate him I and my three brothers never knew a moment of boredom. It was, however, my mother who ruled us all. She deliberately set about creating a close knit family, bound together by shared interest and jokes, a common language and a togetherness which would survive the shocks of the modern world. She did not approve if we upset the police by our behaviour in our cups, but she continued to love us all. She could control any child, however spoilt and wild, and could teach the most backward and difficult, devoting from six o'clock to seven every day to lessons with a quiet but iron discipline. I never heard her raise her voice.

Outside the house, these very square parents had the wisdom to give us complete freedom during the long holidays, when we swam, roamed the hills and fished, learned about nature, and battled with each other on tennis courts, squash courts, cricket and rugby fields. The presents they gave us were always creative: encyclopaedias, squash rackets, chemistry sets, skates, painting equipment. Such freedom, when we could hitch hike and wander the hills all day, is hardly possible today.

Feminism, however overdue and welcome, has done much to undermine such powerful matriarchy. In the extended family she created, she passed on happiness, order and a form of immortality. From beside my brother's gin cupboard her portrait looks down with one eyebrow faintly raised, and many a male descendant has in consequence changed his mind about a refill. When our children and our children's children return in their holidays and laugh and enjoy themselves, I owe it to my parents, as well as to a wife with a genius for friendship, communication and understanding.

In a world which rejects so many of these values, and mocks the institution of family, it was a longing to pass on and to share that happiness that gave me an urge to be a teacher and - more dangerously - to write. So here it is, for better or for worse.

One plea to my readers. Please make allowance for the fact that some of the articles were written 30 years ago: even dinosaurs change!

L.B.L.
1996

Youth

Fun and Games

I must have been a tiresome little boy, less athletic than my brothers, with curly fair hair and blue eyes: a wimpish Fotherington-Thomas: 'Hullo sun! Hullo sky'; a loner who didn't like parties or boys who played rough games. Loving classical music, talking French and flooring adults with statistics and dates, I tended to go skippety-hop and to sing before breakfast, like that Hilaire Belloc character who 'was quite unnaturally keen on *Athalie* by Jean Racine.'

Asthma held me back, physically, until the school Doctor cured me by making me think I was macho and adult. While other boys were having radio malt, virol or cod liver oil, he made me drink a pint of Whitbread's every morning at eleven. It worked, purely psychologically, I suspect. I grew 6 inches in a year, however, and eventually became co-ordinated; my brothers then locked me in a squash court to practise, and I went to a gamesy school. Eventually I beat one of my three elder brothers at something, fell in love with games and lived happily ever afterwards.

As a Headmaster I learned that Other Things count. I would, however, consult the school rugby coach (Tony Cuff!) before Prizegiving. 'Are you going to produce an unbeaten team, Tony, or shall I have to bang on about the greater importance of music, art and technology?'

The day of the worship of the 'Games Blood' has rightly gone. A good eye for a ball, leisure and a good physique don't necessarily qualify people for well-paid, responsible jobs. Some never grew up enough to tackle the real life for

1

which they believed team games were a preparation. They became parasitical, booze-thickened bores, with no ideas or conversation beyond memories of the not very distinguished feats of their distant youth.

Yet there were also all-rounders of great charm and wide interests, men who were deeply immersed in important jobs, but reserved their week-ends for practising sport. Often very talented, they were humorous, friendly and sportsmanlike. There was a lifelong camaraderie which may never be quite recaptured in the ferocious atmosphere of modern professional sport.

How lucky I and my three brothers were. Our mother was devoted to Dad. Sex, Religion and Fundamentals were seldom mentioned in the home. Although we sometmes wondered how they had brought us into the world, their Victorian standards and their quiet example were a powerful influence. It was a remarkably harmonious household, thanks largely to our extraordinary freedom to go where we pleased and to fill the days with our hobbies and games. She ruled the family with ease and firmness. No child ever queried her decisions, although her voice was never raised. One eyebrow would be faintly twitched, or she might say : 'Dear Man would not like that!' We knew that Dad had never expressed any such opinion.

Always pretending to lack the many talents of her husband, she had, on the quiet, a formidable intelligence, speaking excellent French and German, reading widely, especially history, and being a profound observer of the human scene. She was a genius at teaching children and grandchildren, and frequently came to the rescue of unhappy pupils and, indeed, of their parents.

Because our father was a brilliant all-rounder and because he was a public school master, we had the best tuition, all the facilities, and long holidays in which to enjoy them. He passed on to all of us the priceless gift of enthusiasm. We overdid it; but it would have been a crime not to take full advantage.

Our sporting obsessions did not prevent work. At Sedbergh there was half an hour of early morning prep, lessons from 9 to 1 with a twenty-five minutes break, more lessons for an hour and a half in the afternoon, lessons on Saturday mornings (usually cut short by matches) and two and a half hours of homework under strict conditions of silence in the evenings. No home week-ends or half-term holidays.

There were breaks, however, extra half holidays and Sundays. The house yard, enclosed in high walls, gave us opportunity for practising every kind of game. Our shoes were rapidly ruined by yard soccer and cricket, and by practising drop and place kicks. In free time we escaped into the countryside to fish, to watch birds, to climb the crags and to bathe in the deep, clean and rocky pools.

In the holidays, our rivalry was intense. I was the youngest. John, the eldest and biggest, was good at tennis and rugby, useful at squash and cricket, and, later on, at real tennis and golf. Elder-brothermanship and crafty gamesmanship made him as redoubtable at darts as at rugby, at which he captained an unbeaten Rugby School XI, St. Andrew's University and the Rugby Lions. He would, I think, have been capped for Scotland, but for the war. He became a man of distinction and kindness, very much the Head of the clan.

Dad still played competitively with us in his forties. An international at rugby and cricket, he kept up with all the latest techniques, and introduced us to the joys of fishing and painting. Rab, the second brother, quick as a trout, whose international career was cut short by the war, had a marvellous instinct for going one way and sending opponents the other. He was totally unselfish and devoted a lot of his time to raising me towards his standards. He was the first rugby player I ever saw kissed on the field; when he scored the winning try in the last second of the County final, Harold Wheatley, the English second row forward, picked him up like a doll and hugged him. In squash, especially, we competed on level terms for some 20 years, and when he left for New Zealand our final match was declared a draw at 2 all. He became a Public School Head like me. I was ambitious for my school, but this ambition was seasoned with a pinch of hypocrisy and a touch of showmanship. Rab just concentrated on being a good man and on upholding the Right with grace, humour and modesty. In this he succeeded marvellously.

Paddy, the third brother, had a tubercular knee joint, resulting in a permanently stiff right leg. He acquired compensating strength in his arms and wrists, swam, danced and played cricket, tennis and squash. He taught himself to fence very successfully - left handed, so that he could lunge on to his sound left leg. His manual dexterity and his experience of suffering enabled him to become a distinguished surgeon of rare judgment, humanity and courage.

We were shamefully privileged. We swam before breakfast in the holidays, and then competed at gymball, discus and shot, tennis or squash, or practised rugby or cricket. We came in two hours later drenched in sweat and glowing with contented exhaustion, to share a huge bath with wooden surrounds amply provided with floating ducks and boats and with ample spaces for a pint of cold beer. Later the fun Rab and I had with London Scottish was riotous.

What is there about male youth which makes games so exciting? The delight of a well-timed side step, the thrill of disguising the direction of a drop shot so well that even the oldest opponent is foxed, the rare exhilaration of a perfect stroke? Is it a comparatively harmless way of getting rid of aggressive warrior instincts?

It was, doubtless, a waste of time which should have been devoted to

3

righting the wrongs of the world. Some say that sport is only for the big, the strong, the fast and the successful. I don't think that is true. We enjoyed our bad golf enormously, and even a game of shove ha'penny, which makes no demands on talent or physique, was fun and drama.

I am glad I misspent my youth playing games. It may be childish to enjoy directing a ball with cunning and success or deceiving opponents, or to chase desperately around to try to stretch a better player, but it harms no one, makes one feel good and promotes friendship and laughter. It is better than watching the telly and less damaging than most of the other activities to which we later devote our leisure hours. Although in old age we love spending time on music, painting, writing and fishing, most of us would give anything to be able to recapture the exhilaration of an hour on a squash court or rugby field in our twenties.

Heaven or Hell?

Cold baths every morning, a daily run up Winder (1,554 feet) before breakfast, unheated dormitories with windows wide open throughout the winter, an average of twelve inches of rain in the first half of October, inhospitable dayrooms, furnished only with wooden benches, tables and lockers, a stark choice between rugby or runs up the fells every afternoon, a cross-country race which took us up to 1,100 feet, down and up again, in snowy conditions for over ten miles, and no shortage of corporal punishment for the backsliders. Former pupil fathers sent their children when their turn came; some mothers, with gentle, poetic or fragile sons, wondered whether a five-year stretch at Dartmoor would be less demanding.

So much for the legend. Was it true or false? If true, why did the dads send their children back?

It was both true and false. Sedbergh, until the late nineteen-thirties, was certainly tough, but even in those days it was a centre of scholarship with a fine artistic and musical tradition. If it had stayed as it was, no doubt Esther Rantzen's telephone would have fizzed and crackled, and the world would have held up its hands in horror. In fact, however, it was thoroughly enjoyed by most boys, and the softer spirit of post-war Britain has long since eliminated the more ferocious aspects. The school motto, *Dura virum nutrix* (stern nurse of men), ensures that pampering is no part of the educational plan, but it was never true that we had to run up Winder every morning before breakfast. Comfortable common rooms and cosy studies were introduced; a modern

4

school doctor of liberal persuasion ended cold baths; and corporal punishment is sliding back into history.

Yes, there was a lot of rugby. Will Carling is only the last of a long line of internationals, English and Scottish, from Wavell Wakefield to the present, who enormously enjoyed first-class coaching and generous encouragement.

Yes, there was a lot of running; but it was in the most beautiful of surroundings. We felt marvellously fit.

Yes, there were open windows in the dormitories and cold baths. Hundreds of old boys will confirm that they soon grew used to it, and that they have never been bothered by cold or uncomfortable conditions ever since.

Yes, the furnishings were scanty. But the classrooms were adequate, the teaching excellent and the supervised silence for the long hours of homework ideal. Choral society, orchestra rehearsals and music rooms with pianos in each boarding house, together with compulsory hobbies on Saturday nights, ensured that games were not the only spare-time occupation. We didn't know what boredom meant.

Games were fun at all levels. It was not only the future stars who took advantage of the wall-enclosed yards provided for each house. There was tennis-ball cricket against the lavatory door, yard soccer, touch rugby, kicking practice and shot-putting - all unsupervised and joyful. Of my many relations from four generations who were there, the one who enjoyed it most, curiously enough, was the least games-minded.

It was the summer and spring terms which brought our greatest happiness. Games were given a less exacting priority and there were free afternoons, periodic extra half-holidays, and Sundays, when the school was wise and liberal enough to release us to disappear into the surrounding countryside.

Off we went according to our interests. To Black Force to see the peregrines, to Cautley Crags via the Calf to see the buzzards and the ravens, to climb the rock face and to marvel at that glorious waterfall. To Dent for a surreptitious pint with a delicious thrill of not-too-wrongdoing. To Danny Bridge to explore the caves. Away to Lord's Dub, a thunderous pool on the Rawthey, eight to ten feet deep, below huge flat rocks. To the salmon pools on the Lune above Water's Meet, to the trout in the delightful little rivers, the Clough and the Dee, or, with special permission from angler-housemasters, to fish for sea trout by moonlight.

It was ultimate bliss and ultimate freedom. The fells and the dales were our Garden of Eden. The Sedbergh fells, Wild Boar Fell, Baugh Fell, the Calf, Higher Winder and the Howgill Fells, were, apart from Baugh Fell, heather, shrub and treeless. The bare hillsides were covered with short, windswept, ochreous grass, which could gleam gold and silver in the sun. Nowhere was

5

out of bounds, nothing forbidden. It would shock modern welfare state mentality, which seeks to wrap us in cotton wool from the cradle to the grave. Rock climbing should be supervised by qualified instructors, no one should swim in a river without a trained lifeguard; it was mad to allow teenagers up into the high hills in the winter. But we were supremely fit, we learnt fast and we became utterly at home. We knew how to follow the becks down to the valleys if caught by mists, we learnt to slide down the wet hillsides on the heel of a gym shoe at tremendous speed, we knew our way among the treacherous rocks of the riversides. There was nobody to waylay us, to rape, to rob, to abuse or murder. The worst thing any villager ever did to us was to offer us instruction in guddling, tickling or noosing trout. If we were exhausted crossing the Calf in a snowstorm, we were revived by high tea at the Cross Keys, with ham as thick as a doormat, two fried eggs and a glass of scarlet Vimto.

We mastered the art of upstream wet fly fishing with partridge and orange and snipe and purple - short line, wading stealthily as herons, quickly striking. We got to know the rich wildlife. In those two marvellous Cumbrian weeks of summer - one in late May and one in early or mid-June - we lay on our backs in the bluebell woods or the buttercup meadows after our swimming or our fishing, listening to the 'tissick' of yellow grey wagtails, or the silvery cascade of notes from willow warblers, and knew that paradise was here and now. If Eve and the serpent were lacking, it was no great loss. One needs one unattainable bliss to feed one's dreams.

It was a gift beyond the means of city schools. It provided us with an understanding of the countryside and a lifetime's joy. Nothing has proved so precious or so lasting.

Wuthering Farm

It was near the beginning of the war. My brother and I had just left school and were waiting to join an Officers' Cadet Training Unit. In the meantime, for twelve long weeks, July to September 1940, we were asked to help our country by working on a farm.

Never shall I forget those months at what I shall call Wuthering Farm - nor the principal characters involved. The farmer was 5 foot 8 inches tall, 63 years old and weighed 17 stone without an ounce of fat. He could take hundred-weight sacks of corn in each hand and swing them simultaneously on left and right shoulders with a deftness and power I have never seen equalled. He was a weather-beaten old rogue of no intellectual pretensions, but of great cunning, personality and worldly wisdom. He viewed the prospects of employing two young ex-public schoolboys without enthusiasm. When first he clapped eyes on our unsuitable clothes, our smooth cheeks and our soft hands, he made no attempt to conceal his mingled scorn and alarm. He had never thought much of the Government, and we were its latest and greatest folly.

He made us rise at 5.30 a.m. and allowed us to stop work at 10.00 p.m. For this we were paid the sum of seven shillings and sixpence a day. We never heard the word 'overtime' and were innocent enough to accept his view that even this amount was an excessive tax on his personal profits. We should, he gave us to understand, be glad to offer our services to our country for no reward. In practice, that is what happened, for on Sundays the old B............ took us down to the pub. Lord, how we looked forward to that expedition; it was the only break we had in the whole week, apart from meals! He made us play dominoes to a set of rules decided by himself. Losers bought the drinks, which, for him, were always double scotches, and we never won. At least this had the merit of putting him in such high good humour that we really thought we were endearing ourselves to him.

His wife was 19 and, to our young eyes, of great and curvaceous attractions. We would come back exhausted and starving after our forced labour in the fields, and she was not above lowering her eyes and flashing profoundly disturbing glances at us from under her long lashes. Moreover (and this was much more important to us) she cooked pigeon pie divinely. However mean the old boy was with his cash, he did not grudge us our food and Betsy saw to it that we got extra. Much though her blonde hair, her soft blue eyes, her trim ankles and her muscular femininity haunted our dreams, we never dared to try to advance our cause; he watched her like a hawk, and we were not only young and comparatively innocent, but we were also mortally afraid of him. I expect that in reality she was, in any case, armoured with virtue and girdled with aplomb.

7

I thought I was unusually fit and strong for a member of the effete bourge-oisie. Like most boys of my age and origins, I had wasted a disproportionate amount of my time on sport. I had just broken the school shot putting record and was insufferably conceited about my physique. My brother and I faced up to the prospect of working with Joss and Job (the two permanent labourers, too old to be called up), with arrogant and ill judged equanimity. They were two dark, slow, quiet men, tolerant and even monosyllabically kind. They looked Spanish and might, like many of their kind, have been any age from 35-70. They never laughed at us, indeed we never saw either of them laugh at all, though once or twice we caught a certain look in their eyes.

We were much bigger than them and twice as heavily built, for all our youth. Their accent, indeed their language, was so outlandishly peculiar, even to ears attuned to broad Yorkshire, that we had the utmost difficulty in understanding them on the rare occasions they opened their mouths. Similarly, our plummy voices and multisyllabic observations meant little to them. Communication was not their thing. Years of brutal toil for their formidable master had made them into marvellous work machines who lived for little else. Yet I do not think it was just sentiment that made us feel that in their rhythm and harmony with nature, their silent mastery of this work and in this dignified simplicity, there was an element of poetry - even though they were so outwardly short of ideas and intelligence, so gnarled and withered by toil. Neither had ever been more than a dozen miles from his home.

When we got down to work with them, they acquired a new stature and respect in our eyes. How we worked! On alternate mornings, I had either to muck out the cow byre and milk the cows by hand, or to catch the horse in a vast paddock and somehow connect it up to the cart. Mucking out the byre was the lesser evil for me. I was not brought up on horses and this one was a master of non-violent, non-cooperative resistentialism. When it finally condescended to let itself be caught, it persisted in cropping my hair, which admittedly has always been somewhat hay-like. It took particular delight in humiliating me before Job's faintly sardonic gaze.

At 7 a.m. we went back to a tremendous breakfast. Then out into the fields, either weeding 400 metre rows of dew-soaked root crops (a useless pastime which broke my back), or working on the harvest. Scything oats is all right if you've got rhythm and are experienced. We tried to keep going by memories of Levin in that wonderful scene in Anna Karenina. Unfortunately it was not quite like that. We bound the wheat and stacked it by hand, another skill which did not come quickly. In feverish determination to hide our awkwardness and our exhaustion from Joss and Job, we went at it like bulls. When Betsy brought us our lunch, it was the most marvellous relief of our young lives, and we fell upon it ravenously. Later we loaded the cart with sacks as setting sun turned to harvest moon. Beautiful it was, but we were barely conscious. We unloaded thirty sacks each, carried them up the long ladder and emptied them into the loft. It was an effort which took every remaining ounce of our courage and strength. I sweated and ached all over as, breathless and prickly, I lurched and staggered my way through the last four or five sacks. Joss and Job went quietly on their way, beautifully balanced and without strain, shifting the great weights with utter ease. When we got to bed, there were no dreams. We were so unable to stop that one night I caught my brother in a dazed half sleep stacking his pillows in the middle of the floor.

At the end of three months, I got my call up papers for the army. We were both a little nearer to being men. Never again have I been so fit. Nothing that Sandhurst or the Army could do to us ever approached that training. Neither of us has ever criticised a farm worker since.

On the last night the old boy took us down to the pub again. He allowed himself to be beaten at dominoes for the first time, winked at us and actually said: 'Tha' didn't work bad after all.' It was the highest and most treasured praise I've ever heard in my life. Although after the first week we could cheerfully have murdered him, when we heard, a year later, that he had died of a sudden heart attack, we were genuinely and deeply upset. They don't make many like him nowadays.

The Matchless Sport

In between the hammer blows that Fate inevitably deals us, life has many delights to offer: friendship, painting, wine, music and love.

Why does Gareth Edwards, perhaps the greatest scrum half ever to play for Wales, say that he would rather hook, play and land a salmon than score a try at Cardiff Arms Park? Are anglers mad to devote so much time and passion to this smelly, cruel, boring and uncomfortable sport?

It is only those who have never experienced fly fishing who are dismissive. Try it and see. Friendship changes, the best games are restricted to youth, painting is enthralling but almost impossible, wine can be overdone and love is

9

evanescent, beyond control and certainty. Music is a great consolation.

Fly fishing, however, has everything. It has the skill and physical challenge of the best games, but can accompany us, as Winston Churchill said of painting and might have said of music, to the end, or nearly to the end of the road. It demands full concentration, so that all worldly worries drop away. It takes us to the most beautiful places in the world, an English chalk stream in May or a Highland loch in September, where we work in harmony with Nature. It puts us back in contact with fundamentals, bringing the magical healing of the music of the waters and the liveliness of riverside wild life. It demands wide interests and cunning: the angler has to understand every aspect of trout behaviour - how trout see, how they feel, when they are hungry, where they lie, when and under what circumstances they breed most successfully. He must know something of weather and temperature of air and water, he must know about insect life, waterside plants, birds and beasts. It helps if he is a technologist, a safe expert on knots, a judge of the floating or sinking qualities of leaders and lines. There are countless scholarly byways: the study of water with its surface tension, its P.H. levels, its oxygenation, its temperature, pollution and the cures for pollution, its effects on living organisms; the art of fly-tying; the repercussions of climate in all its aspects; the whole extraordinary business of migration to the sea and back and the mystery of feeding or not feeding by salmon and sea trout freshly returned to the rivers.

Yet the greatest pleasures of fly fishing do not come from all these fascinating studies. They lie in finding the hungry trout at the right time, presenting the right fly in the right way, striking at the right moment, playing it with the right degree of pressure, netting it gently and without fuss. The moment when you see the trout rise to your fly is as exciting as a successful side step, a well timed cover drive or sinking an approach shot at golf. There is, however, one difference. The excitement continues through the whole time that the fish is running, jumping, making for the weeds, threatening to go down the waterfall, diving under the boat, sending messages of power and struggle back through line and rod to your wrist, arm and heart. Nothing makes the adrenalin flow more strongly. No wonder anglers have been found dead of heart attacks with a salmon still on the end of their lines.

Cruelty? The trout is a cold-blooded animal with a hard mouth. It is not likely that a small fly-hook in that hard gristle hurts very much. Many are returned unharmed. Those selected for the grill are despatched more swiftly than those caught in nets, or than animals from the slaughter house, which most of us eat without a second thought.

In all things the supreme excellence is timing, said a Chinese sage. Certainly it is the essence of successful angling. The right time of the year, the right time of day, the infinitely subtle timing of a good cast, the timing of the strike, the timing of your lunch, the timing of your playing of the fish, the timing of your rowing.

Easy! Get your timing right, choose the right fly and off you go.

It should be a doddle, but it isn't, because Nature conspires to defend the trout. Biting winds, stinging hail, drenching rain. If the weather should chance to be agreeable, you will be plagued by clouds of vicious midges and treacherous green-eyed clegs. The best fishing is protected by inaccessibility: approach marches across bogs or through head high nettles, or up steep hills through deep heather and bracken. Let no one underestimate the British jungle. Once you've reached the water the wading can be mortally dangerous. Anglers are drowned every year: the rocks are large and slippery, the currents powerful, and sudden shifts in depth can fill your waders and roll you out of your depth. Overhanging trees and weeds and gusting winds can make trouble for the most skilled, and numb hands can find disentangling fiendishly difficult. To fish three miles of highland river or to handle one of those tubby loch boats in a gale can tax even the young and the fit.

Why then do we persist? Suddenly - if only rarely - the wind softens and a gentle sun warms our backs. The trout go mad, or preparation and timing are perfect, the fly lands within an inch of the target as gently as a butterfly's kiss, and a large trout takes it. All troubles are forgotten, all aches banished, and Heaven comes to earth.

Old age makes it hard to take on the full range of fly fishing's physical challenges, but it brings cunning and teaches us short cuts. We no longer waste time and energy fishing where trout are not lying or at times they are not feeding. The occasions when everything comes right increase, and the difficulties fade. Experience makes up for the loss of our ability to vault over stiles, to bend under branches or to defy strong currents. We think more, rest more often and catch more fish.

By steeping ourselves in the ancient simplicity of the hunt, the wounds inflicted by the often nastier conflicts of civilisation are healed. In skill, excitement and beauty, there is nothing better.

The War

Over fifty years ago! Ageing minds filter out inconvenient memories. I might be able to work out where I was and what I was doing in the second week of January '45 after much research, but it would hardly constitute reliable evidence.

A few startlingly vivid mental pictures remain.

The grim announcement of the war on the radio in my father's drawing room at Sedbergh. I was 17 years old and had been blissfully happy: we had the feeling that all security had vanished. Remembering the terrible accounts of the first world war, we wondered how many of us four brothers would be left after 4 years.

A farcical night out with the school corps and home guard in pursuit of a non-existent German parachutist, which was more Captain Mainwaringish than the writers of 'Dad's Army' ever conceived.

First parade at Sandhurst. Major Tom Harvey's white pekinese. The marvellous drill demonstration by three company sergeant majors. The voice of the R.S.M. 'You're Sir to me, Sir, and I'm Sir to you, Sir, and don't you bloody well forget it, Sir!' and later the voice of another R.S.M. drilling the young officers: 'Mister My Lord Marquis Blandford, Sir, you're marching like a ruptured rook, Sir!'

Light-hearted training in England, drinking and practical jokes, girls and irresponsibility.

V1's and V2's in Croydon where I was doing an armoured car waterproofing course prior to the invasion. People knew where the V1's were going to fall, because the engines shut off before they plunged to earth, followed by a cloud of dust and smoke. With the V2's there was no warning and so no fear: either you were hit, or you weren't.

My unit joined the invasion forces somewhat late. Armoured cars went in front of armoured divisions, once a breakthrough had been made, to see what lay ahead. They were not expected to fight against strong opposition, just to move forward down a pre-arranged route in a series of flat out dashes and pauses, during which the landscape ahead was scanned carefully through binoculars, until the enemy was contacted. We had to try to identify how the opposition was armed. If it was the usual disorganized and demoralised rabble, we might push on. If tanks or anti-tank guns were involved, we reported it to headquarters, hoping that we would not be told 'just niggle round the corner and find out if it really is an 88.'

We withdrew before dusk to a safe harbour area a mile or two behind trouble, where the 'corporal of horse' had strong tea and a good meal for us. We cleaned our guns, netted our wireless sets, went to get our orders for next morning, passed these orders on to our troops, and slept well under canvas stretched from the side of our armoured cars.

Periodically we had a day or two off and would play racing the aces in a barn. Some officers had great experience of racing and worked out the odds as bookies and bookies' clerks like lightning. Quite large sums were exchanged, which did not seem significant at the time! I have a picturesque memory of officers perched ten or fifteen feet up on bales of hay like chickens peering down in a circle at the two key figures handling notes on the floor by torchlight.

The basic unit was a troop: A leading scout car with a driver and a gunner-scout, two turreted armoured cars, each with a driver, a gunner-radio operator and a commander, and a 'get away' scout car with a gunner and driver, whose enviable duty was to escape and to report what had happened if things went wrong.

We started off in the mornings an hour before dawn to contact the enemy at first light. Since the enemy were in retreat and badly disorganised, enormous deeds of heroism were not called for by this time. The disadvantage was that we were always first down the road. You never quite knew what lay ahead ... mines, tanks or anti-tank guns or scattered infantry anxious to surrender. It was a nervous business. Mines especially are not always easy to see. Fortunately whatever happened happened so quickly that one was too busy to be frightened until afterwards. The 10 seconds after one has been shot at are long practised chaos. My part was unheroic. My favourite weapons were the smoke bombs which covered our prudent retreats: our main aim was to survive now that the war was clearly going to be won.

During the 'Sitzkrieg' after Arnhem and before the crossing of the Rhine we were made to do foot patrols, for which we were ill trained. I remember going along one side of a thick country hedge where we spotted a similar sized patrol of Germans coming up the other. We listened to them talking in whispers, quite unaware that we were only 5 yards away. They stopped and turned back. We decided not to throw a grenade, and merely chalked it up as a victory in a silly, nerve racking game of 'I spy'.

I killed a few Germans. It didn't make me feel as guilty as I ought to have. Even if you are on the attack you feel as if you were firing in self-defence, but it is an evil business.

War is utter confusion. Generals move flags on maps, but soldiers don't know what's happening. Nobody is efficient, not even the Germans. You drive round a corner and four Germans are frying sausages by the roadside. It takes half a minute before anyone can train a gun on anyone, and by then a white flag is usually waved.

I remember answering the call of nature 50 yards from my car. When my trousers were well and truly down, mortar shells began to land around me. Without adequately securing my trousers, I made a dash for the security of armour. My driver briefly raised his hatch to examine my plight. 'Good luck!' he shouted, and then, less loud, 'on your way, bare arse!'

13

I remember helping my scout car N.C.O. to look for mines on a bridge. It was O.K. Before we crossed I scanned the countryside beyond. A large fox trotted across the heath and paused in the sunlight 50 yards away. A thrush sang.

I remember sitting on the turret of my car on a hill top looking around the countryside through binoculars. My headphones were round my neck and I heard: 'Hello, Gela 1. Limejuice coming 1305 figures 261, 482'. Something seemed familiar about the figures. I glanced at my watch: 13.01. I checked the figures: they were a map reference for where my car was. Limejuice was the code word for air support. It took us less than a minute to pack up and hide in the woods a couple of hundred yards below the hill top.

We were just in time. The hill top was devastated by a squadron of typhoons. Some ass in a tank behind us had reported us as 'German armour occupying hill top!'

War is a madness which we must learn to eliminate. In some strange way it taught us togetherness and made us understand that every breath is a joy and a privilege; life was in a new proportion. But Belsen was something else. It was a revelation which has affected me all my life. As long as man is capable of such brutal and incomprehensible inhumanity, we must be always on our guard. My grannie was German and I am deeply affected by Schubert and Wagner. At the end of the war I returned to Cambridge to study German and French literature and history in order to try to understand.

Such understanding must be a part of education everywhere.

Travel by Train

It is sad that so many of us are reduced to advertising for friends, partners or spouses. In a different way it was sad in the Good Old Days, when, in most of the world finding a wife or husband was primarily the concern of parents and family. In France marriages were arranged with an eye to the family property and fortune. If interests were shared, friendships maintained and a common background honoured, so much the better. Love was quite another, irrelevant matter. Out of all this grew a cynical acceptance of adultery, and the French novel. In Jane Austen's England, any male of property and moderate income was besieged by mothers of daughters under 27, who after that age were virtually on the shelf. China, India and Africa all had similar kinds of arrangements. Love outside marriage might be tolerated or punished, but marriage was a more serious matter, needing parental guidance.

Distasteful as it seems, it generally worked better than what is happening now.

Suddenly marriage is out of fashion in Britain. Cohabitation is in vogue without church promises, scraps of paper, community of interests, or consideration of finances and property - or even, at times, of friendship. There is nothing but love to keep pairs together.

This is not a recipe for enduring relationships, nor is it helpful to the welfare of any resultant children. Interests diverge. He gets bored, or frightened at the prospect of responsibility. She gets impatient for her own career, or for a child, or both. It usually ends in disillusionment.

Where, then, should young men and women who are truly interested in a life-long partnership look? In the social round? God forbid! In fashionable bars or discos, or in mainly one sex work places? Dicey in the extreme! No wonder so many advertise.

I have no talent as an agony uncle, for my experience is irrelevant and I am old. My wife and I celebrated, not long ago, our golden wedding after half a century of very happy marriage. If you want to follow our example, try taking a train.

It was in war time, and I was returning as an extremely young officer, from leave. I took the most unglamorous L.M.S. train from Oxenholme to Crewe and then Euston. The train was grimy and smelt of soot. The corridors were packed with tired people in uniform. The windows were steamed up; there was a smell of cheap cigarettes, and fog billowed in every time a door opened; jolting delays were making us late. I was in cavalry uniform with riding breeches, which was misleading, as I knew something about armoured cars, but nothing about horses.

She was also flying under false colours: wearing an unusually smart civilian two piece, and travelling in a first class compartment on a second class ticket. Her extraordinarily beautiful long legs seemed to go on for ever, and she had amazing eyes. A relation of dragonly appearance, who turned out to be a godmother, was sitting beside her, eyeing me with disfavour.

The miles went by in silence, but not entirely without communication. Determined not to lose her, I was puzzled about how to embark on preliminary skirmishes, under the formidably supervised circumstances. By the time we reached Crewe, I could contain myself no longer. Greatly daring, I underlined some passages of the book I was reading ('*Grantchester and other poems*' by Rupert Brooke), handed it to her and said: 'These are my favourite lines, which are yours?'

This may have been the origin of the expression 'shooting a line'. To my delight, she responded.

It was a miracle of love at first sight, which glowed through a studiously ordinary conversation, overheard in every detail by six obviously intrigued other occupants of the compartment.

There must be a 'divinity which shapes our ends'. We shared a taxi on arrival at Euston, and she left me name, address and telephone number in my copy of Rupert Brooke.

A fortnight later, without collusion or wangling, we were posted to the same small town: I in the army and she in the W.A.A.F.S. The odds must have been longer than those against winning the national lottery.

That was it. Five children and a happy half hundred years later, it is clear that it was the best thing I ever did. I could hardly have known that she would be brave, determined, overflowing with generosity and with a genius for friendship and communication - although her curvaceous shape and the turn of her ankle may have offered a hint.

It was just luck.

So forget all that guff about arranged marriages or advertisements; try travelling by rail.

The First Daze of Peace

The Editor of the O.G. Newsletter asked me to give an account of what I was doing on V.E. day: a plain effort to put his ex-Headmaster on the spot.

It is a potentially embarrassing question; not every corner of the Sardine Tin of our early lives should be scraped. It was, however, 50 years ago. Few witnesses are left, and I am too old to care what I say, or to remember the truth with reliable clarity. Memories of the war are now strange; there are a few vivid pictures of which every detail is imprinted for ever, followed by long periods of which we can remember little or nothing, just as war can produce brief times of searing fear or excitement and long stretches of boredom.

Ask me, as Sherlock Holmes might do, where I was and what I was doing on the afternoon of April 3rd, 1943, and I would not have the slightest idea.

But I do remember clearly the somewhat disreputable way in which I spent V.E. day minus one, apart from the feeling of enormous relief which swept over us all, in spite of the shadow of unfinished business in Japan.

I was serving with the 2nd Household Cavalry, who were the reconnaissance unit for the Guards Armoured Division. We were near Cuxhaven in the peninsula between Bremen and Hamburg. Our lightly opposed drive across North Germany was over, and we had reached the sea at the entrance to the estuary of the Elbe river.

The Major commanding our squadron called us together and told us that Germany's unconditional surrender was to be announced the next day. Unfortunately we had temporarily outrun supplies, so that there was no available booze to help celebrations.

He then turned to the wines officer, and asked him to go, with me as interpreter, to see what could be done.

So we went off in a scout car to Hamburg, which had just fallen, and was barely an hour's drive away. The car was stuffed with cigarettes and tinned food, of which we had plenty, in the hope that we might use them as a bargaining currency if we could find a drink shop.

We should have known better. Hardly any recognisable and functional shop was left in Hamburg. There were few walls standing and even fewer roofs.

Although we had expected something of the kind, we were quite unprepared for the eerie emptiness of that huge, desolate city.

Where was everyone? Here and there isolated figures were searching through the rubble and ruins. There was one ramshackle, improvised barter market where a very few people were haggling over a little food and no drink. Most people were lying low in the cellars, half hiding, half waiting, and all wondering what the next hours would bring. Many had fled to find friends or relatives in country towns and villages, and many were dead. Of drink shops there was not a sign; but when we got near the docks we saw, like a candle in the darkness, the unexpected sight of a clearly drunken sailor.

I tried him in German, and then in English to find out how he had achieved his happy state: he understood nothing. He was sufficiently well-oiled to be unafraid and anxious to please. Eventually he replied in fluent French. We didn't bother to ask what on earth he was doing in these unusual circumstances; it was more important to discover how he had come by his drink.

We had struck oil. In response to a few cigarettes, he took us down to the docks. There, abandoned, was a large cargo ship. 'Voilà,' he hiccupped, 'servez-vous!' The most that we could find out was that the contents were destined for the German High Command, and that the German crew had left it about a week ago because of the news. Perhaps because there was so much else to think about, or possibly from some remnants of Teutonic discipline, only a few cases had been taken.

An inspection showed that there were hundreds of cases: Pommard, apricot brandy and Champagne.

A remnant of caution led us to worry that we might be guilty of looting. So, in true army fashion, we passed the buck. We consulted the Major by wireless, he got on to the Colonel, and the Colonel got on to the General. Never was red tape more swiftly cut. Within an hour we had instructions to guard the boat and to requisition the contents. Three tonners were sent. One was filled exclusively for the use of our unit. As a result, if I remember right, we drank Pommard for six old pence a bottle, apricot brandy for three pence a nip and Champagne for one shilling a bottle - for the next six months. No personal profit, but much acclaim.

At the end of a war something snaps. I was 24. Those six months were not the most sober, responsible or creditable in this very junior officer's career, but certainly the most educative. It was quite a relief to return to Cambridge under the 'early release' scheme for those whose University courses had been interrupted by the war.

Looking back on it, I felt that much my most appreciated contribution to Britain's war effort might at least have been rewarded by a mention in despatches. It now seems like a bizarre dream.

Family Life

Growing up is Hard to Bear

There were two little bears who lived in a wood
And one of them was Bad, and the other was Good...
...And then quite suddenly, just like us
One got Better and the other got Wuss...

(A. A. Milne)

How true! Every experienced parent or teacher becomes periodically convinced that one or other child is entering a phase of irreversible decline. However much educational pundits draw smooth upward graphs, marked by regular tests at seven, 11, 14, 16 and 18, progress is and always was an incalculable sequence of fits and starts.

Puppy fat at 18 months, skin and bones at six, pre-adolescent pudginess at 12, spotted bean pole at 15 - the road to 19-year-old beauty is a bumpy track. The path of emotional balance and intellectual sharpness is no less bewilderingly uneven. At times many of us wonder whether we have given birth to a monster or, which is an almost equally dangerous illusion, to a precocious genius.

One can risk a few generalisations about this stop-go process, while recognising that each child is a law to itself. There are hazards for which parents should be - and seldom are - prepared.

First, there is a marked difference between the sexes in the age at which

19

they develop. Girls are generally more conscientious and often brighter until about 13. They get through the muddle of adolescence earlier and emerge to achieve a degree of emotional maturity and understanding at an age when their brothers are still in incoherent doldrums.

This contributes to the proven superiority of the girls' academic performance at 16. It is also established that boys catch up at a later stage..

There is another important factor, familiar to all teachers but inadequately researched by scientists. Boys who grow very quickly to become tall in their early mid-teens lose co-ordination of mind, body and emotions for a considerably longer time than their more steady-growing companions. They often lack concentration, are bad at games and suffer from self-consciousness and depression. Eventually they 'grow into' their tall bodies, but may not reach their full potential until 17, 18 or even their early 20s.

Adolescence may be a time when a sensible psychiatrist's help may be needed to combat temporary depression. The familiar sullen, rebellious, silent, difficult stage may indicate that minerals and chemicals are out of balance.

Parents should brace themselves for the possibility of 'all change' after adolescence with both girls and boys. While the hormonal and chemical changes may cause temporary confusion and lack of direction, when adolescence is over, those that were first may be last and vice-versa. Some are galvanised into sudden motivation and even brilliance, some precociously brilliant 11-year-olds finish as mediocrities.

This should be a warning to parents, teachers, selectors, interviewers and employers not to be over-excited or disappointed by results in periodic tests and exams. Of course examinations give helpful evidence and provide indispensable motivation, but they must never be regarded as final and absolute evidence. Above all it is sheer foolishness to pretend that a MENSA rating for a three to five-year-old child should be taken seriously. Remember too that changes of school, quality of teaching, health and motivation can make far more difference to examination results than minor differences in measurements of IQ.

Do not despair when your child changes from whizz kid to jelly-minded nincompoop. Don't exult if she suddenly wins all the laurels. It may all change back in a few years, and by the time she's 30, the cocktail will have shaken down to her own special mixture, in which school exams will only be a small element.

In the meantime just communicate, help and pray.

Dads and Daughters

When your daughter first starts to bring home boy friends, it can be, and usually is, a rude shock.

You may be the lucky dad whose daughter picks a civil, cultured, strong, charming and successful young man, who will play golf or go fishing with you and buy expensive liqueur chocolates for mum. But most of us suffer ghastly years when spotty and speechless boys, apparently devoid of physique, charm or brain, mysteriously exert a magnetic attraction on our beloved and beautiful daughters.

The more devastatingly elegant and charming the girl, the more inevitably she chooses for her first love somebody who, to the jaundiced fatherly eye, looks as though the cat had just brought him in. 'The trouble is,' spluttered a friend, whose pretty daughter was becoming defiantly and undesirably entangled, 'she's a princess, and he's no prince!...barely even a frog,' he added as a charitable afterthought.

Well - I expect the wretched young man was his mother's prince, and my friend's daughter was not every man's idea of a princess. The sad truth is that fathers are jealous and suspicious, and the younger they are the more they suffer. They are, in any case, the worst judges of what is good in very young males, or of what attracts very young females.

Girls may enthuse about 40-year-old smoothies on the screen, and when they reach the twenties they may alarm you by preferring men of double their own age (whose tendency to play golf with you and to buy expensive liqueur chocolates for mum will suddenly become intensely suspect to you!); but their first experience of love is more likely to light on the nearest adolescent. Just because he may look odd to dad, and may be struck dumb by the older generation's clumsy attempts at conversation, father should not conclude that there is nothing to him. Young girls are not so stupid as their fathers think. They realise that a teenager who plays golf with dad and buys mum expensive liqueur chocolates is likely to be a doubtful character, oily and devious. Their wily feminine intuition may appreciate hidden qualities in their young men that have escaped their school teachers or their fathers. Many of the apparently wet adolescents who were the first loves of beautiful girls in their mid-teens turn out in their thirties to be wealthier, better looking, more successful, accomplished and charming than the prefect types that their fathers would have preferred, and who so often later lapse into boring mediocrity. Mothers can also be more perceptive about these things than their husbands. Parents with long memories may remember that their own first ventures met with a chill reception from their elders.

The older-man stage can be trying. A square, games-playing dad of my acquaintance fumed helplessly when his daughter brought back an artist nearer his age than hers. He had hair halfway down his back and a tendency to go skippety-hop and to say: 'My deah!' with a deprecating wave of his soft, long-fingered and excessively well-manicured hand. This was, in fact, a proper punishment for father's restricted horizons. It was very understandable that his daughter should have been driven to this admittedly exaggerated mind-broadening exercise. Dad was unable to speak a civil word to the man, and the family temporarily fell apart.

Fortunately, a gradual change usually takes place after such early shocks. Either parents grow softer and more tolerant with age, or children become more discriminating: probably both. The older generation learns first not to criticise boy or girl friends, and then to like them. It is, after all, a supreme compliment that they are brought home at all.

When parents learn not to feel completely responsible, they reach that closeness which so many grandparents enjoy. When we reach our fifties, we trust our young - or at least recognise that criticism and advice is likely by then to do more harm than good. Our children have learned to love members of the opposite sex for more understandable and sensible reasons. Quarrels about dress, or about returning home in the small hours, and scenes about sleeping together or not, or where, or when, are forgotten. The happy stage may even be reached when dad and mum genuinely love the boy and girl friends and cease to interfere.

The thought may then occur to you that you might well have spared yourselves, parents and children, a great deal of hassle if you had given up the struggle to offer guidance from the beginning - as all you did made no difference anyway.

But you could be wrong. The fact that your advice seems to be ignored or that you are contradicted does not mean that you are without influence. There would be something missing in a family in which there were no hassles in the early stages. For the effort to provide example, gentle criticism and advice (however little heeded) is a symptom of love. Dads and mums who showed no reaction to their children's boy and girl friends and their behaviour would be poor and ultimately unappreciated parents - and their genuine joy and approval of later choices would be the less welcome and convincing.

All in the Stars

I don't go much for astrology. The view of the physics department of Berkeley University makes sense.

Dr Shawn Carlson is reported in *Nature* as announcing in California the results of tests carried out on 300 people whose horoscopes were cast by 28 astrologers recommended by the American National Council for Geocosmic Research. The conclusion, as any fool could have told them, was that there is no evidence that remote heavenly bodies exert any influence on our character. The horoscopes had no greater value than could be expected by chance.

It all reminded me of that splendid character Priscilla in *Chrome Yellow*. This formerly wealthy lady's twin passions were gambling and astrology. Before the Derby and the Oaks, she would cast the horoscopes of every competing horse and jockey, and before filling in her pools coupon would repeat the process for every player of League football. This involved her in analyses of heavenly conflicts of such vast complexity that it was hardly surprising that she lost money in suitcase-fulls throughout the year.

So when my primevally superstitious elder daughter, who, like many of her generation, will neither buy a toothbrush nor accept an invitation unless the heavenly omens are favourable, rang to pass on an important warning, I was just irritated.

The stars made it clear, she said, that there was a bad time ahead for her and for her Dad. As the Inland Revenue had just achieved the unthinkable by sending me a cheque, unexpected and unasked, for £175 on my birthday, I was not impressed, and brushed her advice aside.

Next morning I headed happily North to give a quite well-paid lecture in Ayrshire. After barely five miles, I pranged my car, skidding on wet leaves and mud and doing £2000 worth of damage. Hiring another at great expense, not met by the insurance company, I got to the lecture after driving through a snowstorm, with rising blood pressure, behind four 'Long vehicles' from Dumfries to Ayr.

On my return I heard that my daughter's flat had been burgled, and all her jewellery and a large part of her cash savings, destined to pay for a forthcoming move, stolen.

Not good. My wife was away. In order to create some good news to soften the bad, I determined to keep an overdue promise to cut the ivy which was swallowing up both house and barns. I worked in a frenzy until it was dark. In the gathering gloom I destroyed the Virginia creeper, which my wife had been cultivating for 12 years, and severed the television ærial cable in two places.

At this point the phone rang. Running into the dark entrance hall in order to get there before it stopped, I caught my foot in the lead and tore it from the control box. The phone clattered on to the tiles and was shattered. All communication was effectively destroyed.

My wife was very understanding, but I thought it would be prudent to butter her up. So I agreed to go to the tailor with her to buy myself a new suit, which she had long urged me to do. Just before going, we learned that another suit we had ordered for my son had never reached him - lost in the post.

My own post included another letter from the Inland Revenue asking me this time to pay back the sum they had sent to me on my birthday.

The shopping expedition was a shade gloomy, and I must have been preoccupied. Everyone else was parking on the single yellow line, and it was a one-way street with plenty of room. Somehow or other the parking ticket did not seem quite just. If I told the traffic warden the whole story, would she relent? Unmoved and incorrupt, she did not.

I went home, bought no shopping, and determined to stay indoors, move nowhere and undertake no financial transaction until the curse should be lifted.

It's not that I believe in astrology; the fault, Dear Brutus, is not in the stars, but in ourselves. Unfortunately that is small comfort. The realisation of one's crass incompetence is not cheering.

What I look forward to least of all is the sight of that ill-disguised expression of triumph which will flit across my daughter's face when next she comes home. I know she loves me, but there is nothing like being able to say, 'I told you so.'

Yours Truly

'Dear Mummy and Daddy, We lost to Town Close today 3-1. Had a mingey fowl breakfast. Please send me a yott. Love and kisses...'

I've always thought that authentic letter, from a nine-year-old at boarding school, exemplary. Clearly uncensored, brief and straight to the point, it included a report on the essential things that had gone wrong, a request that didn't beat about the bush and an expression of affection.

Girls, as in some other respects, are more indirect, subtle and literate as correspondents. Relationships and hardships are hinted at, direct requests don't figure so frequently. They are liable to invent codes, to resort to invisible ink and to indulge in fantasies.

The one I like best was the letter from a daughter who had disgraced herself by 10 weeks of ominous silence.

'Dear Mum, I'm afraid I've got some rather shattering news for you. Please break it gently to Dad, I dare not tackle him myself. Right at the beginning of term we had a fire in the dormitory. No one was burned, but it was a bit of a fright. I was rescued by such a splendid looking fireman that I fell hopelessly in love. Things hadn't been going too well, and when he returned with his ladder one night, I eloped with him. I'm now living with him in a tiny flat in town. The really bad news is that I'm expecting a baby and have now found out that he is married with two children...perhaps you can understand why I've been scared to write.

P.S. It's OK, really. None of the above is true, but I failed French O-level again, and just thought you ought to get it in proportion. Love, Sal.'

As accomplished letter-writers get older, they tend to split into two camps: the short, polished, witty ones and the long ones which tell all, like those professional telephone talkers whose full hearts know no cash limits. In the first category I treasure a letter to the *Daily Telegraph* from R. Neville of Crowborough.

'Sir, Mrs Thatcher is quite right to condemn the unhygenic custom of baby-handling by electioneering parliamentary candidates.

My son was sitting in his perambulator, harmlessly surveying the sea at Criccieth, when he was patted on the head by Mr Lloyd George. He was bald before he was 30.'

Letters of advice from parents to children may hit the jackpot, but they are usually better burnt before posterity finds them. The Archduke Ferdinand wrote to his Mum to ask whether he should take a young musician into his house. The Empress replied:

'I do not know where you can place him, since I feel you do not require a composer or other useless people. But if it would give you pleasure, I have no wish to prevent you. What I say is only meant to persuade you not to load yourself down with people who are useless...'

The useless person in question was Mozart.

Of all civilized and elegant letters, few can excel that attributed to a Red Indian chief in the History of the Indians of North America in 1834, even though its authenticity is questionable After the treaty with the White Man, the Commissioners of Maryland and Virginia invited the Indians to send their sons to William and Mary College to benefit from the best classical education. This was the reply they received from the supposedly uneducated wilderness.

'Gentlemen, We know that you highly esteem the kind of learning taught in these Colleges and that the maintenance of our young men would be very expensive to you. We are convinced, therefore, that you mean to do us good by your proposal; and we thank you heartily. But several of our young people were formerly brought up at the colleges of the Northern Provinces, they were instructed in all your sciences, but when they came back to us, they were bad runners, ignorant of every means of living in the woods, unable to bear either cold or hunger, knew neither how to build a cabin, take a deer or kill an enemy. They were totally good for nothing.

We are, however, not the less obliged by your kind offer, though we decline accepting it, and to show our grateful sense of it, if the gentlemen of Virginia will send us a dozen of their sons, we will take care of their education, instruct them in all we know, and make men of them.'

Anyone who can pen such a courteous rebuke has little more to learn.

Kid's Stuff

It must be fun to bring joy and laughter to everyone, like John Cleese thrashing his car, when, after a crescendo of Fawlty disasters, it obstinately refused to start.

It is also daunting. Fashions in humour change. Even the wittiest must ration their sallies, work on their skills and change with the times.

Yesterday's gags, which had the audience rocking with laughter, bore today's youth, and continual funniness inevitably palls - at least for wives and close friends. Most of us try to be funny when young, and wisely give it up, except by occasional accident, in later years.

Humour is a strange gift. Some people keep television audiences in fits by saying silly things which are unadulterated corn: they seem funny only because they have absurdly melancholy faces. Clowns still earn a living by losing their trousers, receiving custard pie in their face and falling on their bottoms with ingenious timing: not particularly difficult, although most of us would not care to try.

Perhaps the clowns have the answer. We can all continue to satisfy our urge to amuse, provided we limit our ambition and turn our attention to small children. Not, Heaven forbid, adolescents, but one to five-year-olds, in whom the simplest devices induce endless fascination and delighted chuckles.

Even the most incompetent fathers and grandfathers can master a handful of tricks which pass the baby-sitting hours cheerfully away and earn a completely disproportionate amount of love and gratitude. Few things are more rewarding for less effort.

Yet it is becoming a lost art. Television may be partly to blame. Restive little children, like their parents, are easily hypnotised into passive somnolence by the sight of coloured balls clicking rhythmically around the green baize and disappearing at the will of cue-waving magicians. If ever the machine is turned off, many parents have no idea how to avert tears once their babies are bored with the kisses and the cuddles.

Rack your brains, dads, mums and grandparents, and remember the elementary skills of the days before television. Practise them surreptitiously in your bath. You cannot have entirely forgotten how to waggle your ears, click your double-jointed thumb, raise alternate eyebrows, roll your stomach, imitate a champagne cork popping with forefinger and mouth, wobble your cheeks, pretend to pull off your thumb, make cuckoo calls by blowing into your cupped hands or a loud squawk with a blade of grass between your thumbs.

Can you no longer construct a paper tube with a loose flap to simulate rude noises in response to sucking? What has become of your ability to make card houses of five storeys and paper æroplanes that really loop the loop or float in long graceful circles down from the bedroom window? Is a cat's cradle beyond you? What about a finger-shadow menagerie on the nursery wall with the light behind you? Elephants may now defeat you, but surely you can still manage wolves and bunnies.

Can't you make fountains of bath water rise 18 inches high through your clenching fist? You may not be able, like the Victorians, to whistle the tune of God Save the Queen and hum the bass part simultaneously, but you can learn to click the national anthem and many nursery rhymes with your tongue. Little physical feats easily impress.

Any one of these devices may enable you to rescue a mum with a crying child on a bus or a train. There is no language barrier, even if there is a regrettable chance that an adult waggling his ears and cuckooing in a public place may be quickly led away to seek psychiatric help. Such skills should not be lost however: expectant fathers especially, should go into training or take refresher courses. It is a valuable contribution to the peace of home, more fun than housework and a change from the crossword puzzle. The occasional embarrassment of being caught practising by an adult is a risk worth taking.

Fathers and Sons

After more than 20 years as a Headmaster, one of my saddest experiences has been to witness how often fathers' ambitions for their sons have turned to disappointment, resentment or unhappiness for either or both. Fathers tend to be blind to the danger of wanting their sons to be mirror reflections of themselves with the grubby patches polished up: mothers seem to be much more happy to see their children grow up different and true to themselves.

It can be strongest in ambitions for games. I am the son, nephew and brother of rugby internationals. Although my father was wise enough to hide his hopes for me, when I found that I had inherited some gifts for the game I was aware of strong pressures. In fact I just 'made the grade', and derived much pleasure from the game, but I now believe that if I had had the courage to persist with music lessons instead of rugby training it might have benefited me more in the long run. If I had 'failed' it would have disappointed me ridiculously.

Ambition for one's children often represents the desire to reach through them summits which eluded one in youth. I know a squash coach who has trained his son single-mindedly from childhood to become a champion. The boy is, of course, very good. But he may not reach the top; he may break a leg, or develop faulty eyesight or just not be fast enough. He may even rebel in adolescence and prefer beer or history, girls or physics, art, hockey or even life. If one is not a physical phenomenon, there is a case, nowadays, for playing games in what used to be called a genuinely amateur way: it is reasonable to hesitate before sacrificing unlimited time, money and energy to the achievement of modest success in the second rank in an era when the brilliance of a 16m shot putt by a man of 82kg will make no impact among the 127kg giants, and when a 50 second 400 metres by a 15-year-old is no more than commonplace.

The desire to see sons win academic laurels can be even more dangerous, especially if it is concentrated on father's preferred faculty. As a linguist, I made the mistake of trying to teach my children, who were not making a success of French, myself. Within a few minutes there were floods of tears. Years later, with me and school both safely far away, both my elder children became good linguists. Parents, schoolmasters, and employers attach too much importance to O and A levels. One has only to look at the high table of many an Oxbridge college to realise that academic ability can be spectacularly different from competence.

It is only gradually dawning on us that universities do not necessarily provide the key either to a successful or to a remunerative life. Polytechnics are not only easier to get into, but often more practical and efficient in their courses. 'Below' this, training and rewards can be better still, for academic distinction tends to be the passport to middle class and professional jobs offering heavily taxed salaries, few perquisites and disproportionate obligations and expenses. A three or four O level man often has more business acumen for money making and more human understanding for management. He does not conclude, like the first class honours man, that his education finished at 23 and that he need never think again, but works hard for tangible and productive objectives, learning as he goes.

One cannot run school appeals every seven years without noticing that the bright scholars - of whom we so much approved and whom we made our school prefects - who got their scholarships to Oxford and Cambridge, write back politely and in flawless prose in answer to our begging letters, apologising for the fact that, being in academic jobs, they can only spare a fiver. The rebels and the examination failures, on the other hand, hasten to come to see you, park the Rolls outside your office, diffuse nostalgic affection for the old school and leave a large seven-year covenant.

The truth is that there has been a social revolution in careers. Although the public schools would no longer claim, as in 1966, over three-quarters of the judiciary, the bishops, the diplomats, the physicians, the admirals, generals, air chief marshals and vice chancellors, there are still links with those worlds...Attempts to persuade state schoolboys to apply in greater numbers to the Foreign Office have been only partly successful: a lifetime of hard and uninfluential work for a small power, and a small salary, for the sake of a possible place on some future honours list, is an acquired taste. In response to national need, however, the public schools are now sending a higher proportion of students to engineering, to industry and to business management.

Although the numbers going to university from the public schools have inevitably risen, as the grammar schools went comprehensive, their pupils have understood that financial reward no longer goes to the academic and professional jobs.

Who is rich? It is hard to know, but there is plenty of money around and in surprising places. Arabs, of course, and a few famous tycoons. There are still a few landowners not finally crippled by taxation. But, in my part of the world at least, the middle rich are those who buy and sell for cash in hand, who pay little or no tax and who would never be at a loss for how to produce £20,000, although they have little responsibility and few expenses.

Apart from that, he who was first is often last. The welder earns more than the physics master, the electrician more than the vicar, the carpenter more than the clerk, the pop star than the Prime Minister. The boy who runs away to sea to join the Merchant Navy may earn, before he is 40, twice as much as his M.P.

Much of this is fair, except for the unequal burden of tax which bears too heavily on salaried management and is so easily avoided by the dealer. What is new and exciting is that the schoolboy whose gifts lie in craftsmanship or in business no longer feels that he is pursuing the second best. He thinks hard and long about what he likes doing, and if he prefers being an electrician to being a barrister, parental pressure will not deter him from the happiness he deserves. And to judge from my last account for repairs to the deep freeze, all other things will be added to him.

In Memory of Kirsty

Many years have passed by since my small daughter died in a road accident, but it is only now that I feel able to write about it. I do so in the faint hope that it might help some of the many parents who, every year, suffer in the same kind of way.

I want them to know that the impossible can happen, that ordinary life can return; that you can laugh, and at times forget, and even be happy. It is true that there is still something like a lump of cold metal at the back of your brain and in the pit of your stomach. But there comes a stage when you are no longer overwhelmed by tears of self-pity and horror at every little thing that reminds you of her; nor do you regard this as a form of unfaithfulness to her loving memory.

Ours was the last family you would think of in connection with tragedy. I'd grown up in a big, healthy, boisterous family with a cheerful spirit which I tried to pass on to my children. Somehow this seemed to succeed most with Kirsty. My elder son and daughter were the brainy ones, and the youngest girl, at three, was too small for me to tell.

But Kirsty was as bright as the day is long - outgoing, loving, without any apparent complications in her life. She was an outdoor girl, tall for her age, robustly healthy. I didn't favour her especially above the others. I loved all my children. But perhaps Kirsty crept a little closer to my heart because she, more than the rest, shared my interests. When I can steal time away from my demanding job I go off into the woods and fields to watch birds or study fungi. It was Kirsty who used to hurry to come with me; at seven she could identify almost every bird in our local countryside, and distinguish between edible and inedible mushrooms. I remember those hours we spent together as some of the happiest in my life.

To me, the day when it all ended is still yesterday. She was seven, and very proud of a wonderful school report. So anxious was she to rush home and show it to us that she grew impatient at the slowness of the bus. Instead of waiting for the stop just beyond our house, as she usually did, she bounced off at the one before, so that she could rush on and beat the bus to it. In her impatience, without looking left and right she darted across the road behind the bus and went straight under the wheels of an oncoming car.

The two elder children were away at school. My wife was out shopping, taking the baby with her. So I was alone when the phone rang and a neighbour's voice spoke, in a low and unnatural tone: 'Your little girl has been hit by a car, and she's quite badly hurt. They've brought her to my house. You'd better come quickly.'

At first I simply didn't grasp what he meant, and he had to repeat it. Suddenly I felt ill, and life mercifully changed gear, so that reality became a dream and everything I said or did was purely automatic. All my actions seemed to belong to some other person.

I arrived just after the doctor, an old family friend. When I saw Kirsty my first reaction was one of relief. There was none of the blood and mess that I had feared. Perhaps she wasn't too badly hurt after all. She was lying on the sofa with one leg hanging a little awkwardly over the edge. I wondered if it might be broken, and began to breathe again. If that were all....

There was a faint bruise over one eye and some signs of a bang on her head. She was lying on her back, pale, beautiful, unconscious and breathing rather noisily and uneasily, sometimes taking a deeper breath as if she were about to come round. I had just time to take her in my arms when the doctor said: 'I don't quite like the look of her reflexes in that eye. There could be some brain damage. We must get her to hospital immediately.'

I went in the ambulance with her, and the doctor followed behind in her car. The ambulance attendant, whom I happened to know, looked dazed and worried. I was still trying to tell myself that she had nothing worse than a broken leg, that she would come round any moment and recognise me. I held her hand, kissed her, mumbled little nonsenses of consolation to her, desperately praying and trusting in the power of love. She grew quieter and still, and I thought I felt her squeeze my hand. Now, surely, at any moment, she would be coming round.

Suddenly she gave a little sigh that frightened me unreasonably. I shall remember that sound to my dying day.

'I think she's changed colour,' said the ambulance man. 'We'd better stop and let the doctor look at her.'

The doctor gave her a quick look and said, 'I must give her an injection.'

A few moments later we were at the hospital. As she was gently lifted out of the ambulance she still looked little marked or damaged, but her eyes were now partly open and seemed glazed. I noticed a speck of dust against their bright blue. She didn't blink. Then my world spun round and went lastingly out of focus.

She was hustled away into the interior on a trolley, and I was motioned into a waiting room of some description. I didn't even notice if it was furnished or not. The world seemed yet more distant, and my sensation of being in a trance deepened. One or two figures bustled around and time passed. It could have been seconds or hours. A doctor finally came in.

'I'm terribly sorry, there was nothing we could do; she was dead from injuries to her brain when she got here. Everything possible was done. If she

31

had recovered it might in any case have affected her all her life.'

I must have stared at him, quite unable to cry, or to react or to think, although I had known for some time - since I saw the speck of dust, I suppose. I heard a voice say: 'Thank you for trying,' and realised that it was me.

I then turned to the family doctor and said something like: 'I don't feel very much on the ball. You'd better take charge. What am I supposed to do now?'

'You'd better get in touch with your wife....'

Mercifully the trance persisted, and it was barely me that went through the motions of dialling home. Dreadfully Jo's voice answered.

'I've been told about her being hit,' she said. 'Is it very bad?'

'Very bad,' I replied.

'She's dead, isn't she?' asked the voice.

God knows why, but I think I hesitated a second before saying 'Yes'. I said some other things, but there was nothing else to say.

I went home, and from the nightmare of the next few days there remain flashes which still come back to me with frightening force. The face of the au pair girl coming back from an afternoon off. Someone had told her, and she looked at me with shock and horror, as if I were a being from outer space. I remember relief of a kind as my wife and I talked about it together in the bedroom, and shared our floods of tears at last.

I remember the shock and joy of discovering that our little daughter had written on the wall of the bathroom before she left for school that morning: 'I love you, Mummy and Daddy!' in big clear hand-writing. We were sentimental enough to frame it and to feel that it must have been some premonition or message of consolation.

Then there was the unreal nightmare of dealing with all the practical mummery of death ...choosing the coffin, persuading the rector to let us have a corner of the over-crowded churchyard. The sight of her in the Chapel of Rest, beautiful and fresh as the spring, but cold to my farewell kiss, and with the bruise on her head and face now spread over forehead, temple and cheek, sinister and purple; an unreasonable frenzied belief that love, faith and prayer would somehow work a unique miracle before the coffin lid was closed. Even at the funeral service we prayed as we had never, alas, prayed before, believing that an exception could be made for us, because love and faith can move mountains if strong enough, and nothing could be stronger than ours.

I remember too the bizarre farce of going on with the ordinary and often very public duties of my profession. People in the middle distance would look pityingly at me, or admire my courage, which was still nothing but the indifference of a trance condition. My body and mind continued to function, but I knew that I was, in a sense, dead; beyond the fear of anything which anyone could do. A whole part of me had died; the protected, optimistic, competitive, joyful, hopeful, strong part seemed to have gone for ever. For years afterwards I would keep being gripped by the acute sense of loss and resentment.

When death comes to the aged, however beloved and close, there is time to prepare, a sense of mission accomplished, somehow a feeling of harmony. For the death of a seven-year-old there is no such consoling inevitability. Sudden death at that early stage is an abrupt and intolerable outrage. She was too sweet and too young to have developed any nastiness, and her promise of joy to herself and others seemed without limit.

I remember how, a few weeks earlier, she had demanded that I should atone for using the word 'bloody', when I was dressing in the morning and had lost my collar stud, by standing to attention in my shirt and pants and singing *Holy, holy, holy* three times. I had obliged, and it was the memory of this amusing little incident which made me laugh again for the first time. Gradually, and in a different way, laughter does return.

I survived the inquest somehow, peering curiously at the driver of the car who hit her. I managed to say a few words to him, just to let him know that we didn't blame him in any way for what had happened. He may, or may not, have been travelling rather too fast. I felt only pity for him in his obvious horror and bewilderment.

Now, at last, I can look back, and see things which were invisible for many years. How, for instance, it brought Jo and me closer. We had always had a good and happy marriage, but at the same time I was in the early years of my career. Like many people anxious to be a success, I think I'd let myself get too swallowed up in my professional world. I seldom got back home before eight in the evening. After that there was work to do and interruptions from various people who came to see me. It had left little time for the things that really matter - having a happy home, being with the children, sharing outside interests with my wife. After a life in which we had not given much thought to sharing, we were made to share shatteringly and completely something no one else could understand, something common to us both.

Together we experienced the wilderness of grief, the bitterness, the impotence, the fury, the futility of unanswered prayers. We emerged knowing each other better, stronger in our love for each other, and determined that we should have another child.

It was no accident that Bede was born only 18 months after Kirsty's death. His birth seemed to bring us alive again too. His healing power was everything we had hoped. He was very like her, a happy, marvellous child. And in some ways he really does seem to take her place in the home.

In some ways. That's the crunch. For Kirsty was unique and irreplaceable, as every child is. The loss is still there to be lived with, and, though we try hard not to let ourselves dwell in the past, it always will be.

Both Jo and I are, in our different ways, religious - not orthodox religious, but believers in an intelligent power behind all things. It helps, but not immediately. In the beginning it is impossible to console yourself by believing that all is really well, or that your child is in the bosom of a white-bearded father in the sky. It is only later on that the conviction that some essential spirit has survived becomes a kind of comfort to you.

A bishop, who was an old family friend, wrote us a long letter. He too had lost a beloved child, years before, and had suffered in other ways as few other men have had to. He wrote that in his experience there was no immediate comfort following grief from death. But he also pointed out that it does add a new dimension to life, and in some extraordinary way makes it more worth living, and gives greater value to the passing moments of friendship and attachment.

At the time this letter made no particular impression on me, except that he was being kind. But I have since found out that what he wrote is true. And in fact, as I grew more convinced of the survival of something, the fact that Kirsty had died at the peak of her niceness, at an age when she hadn't had to suffer, or to cut down her ideals or compromise in the way that the middle-aged do, became a marvel that in time I could accept.

I know that this cannot be a comfort to everyone - that there are many who do not share my beliefs. But I know that in the end they too can find peace and acceptance in the world about them; that if they hang on, at first the trance will protect them, and in the end they will share our experience so that more, and not less zest and depth will be brought to their lives. Only those who have known the sharpest suffering can experience the most intense joy.

I still continue to love the countryside and to wonder at the birds and plants that, through me, Kirsty was discovering. I do not try to tell myself that she is - or ever can be - there with me. But I know that it is only because of her that the air is clearer, and my senses infinitely sharper and more aware of everything around me.

I know that out of the despair and bitterness has come much good faith and delight in love and life, the very things that, because of Kirsty's death, I had thought to be gone for ever.

Thank you, little daughter. Perhaps this was your miracle.

Fun and
Games

Sheer Delight

No one is exempt from trouble; yet life has been crammed with sheer delight.

Delight is childhood: who could fail to know it, if they had the good fortune to be carefully and lovingly brought up?

Delight as a young man - particularly in sport. Is there any joy to match rugby at its best played among friends? There are, of course, periodic defeats and humiliations, days of mud, sleet and blood and snide comments from the press. Yet these only serve to increase the fun of the days when the tide flows: the pure exhilaration of the bold anticipation which comes off, the side step which is perfectly timed, the reverse pass that wrong foots the opposition, the patterns woven with team mates at top speed in spring sunlight with the turf taking the strain of your studs and the blood surging through your veins. The memories of laughter, release and good fellowship are golden. It has not always been so, but even today the unique quality of the greatest game of all surfaces and re-emerges to produce dream magic just when one thought it might have perished for ever in the grim faced battles of flying boots and half hidden punches. No rugby player will ever forget every detail of That Try of the Barbarians against New Zealand - little Phil Bennett's three giant side steps, ridiculously undertaken in front of his own posts against the thunderous descent of the entire All Black pack, without a hand laid on him. The sudden flow of electricity passing from him to Gibson and Dawes with their perfect timing, and the final triumphant lung-splitting gallop of Edwards. Every man who touched that ball in that moment achieved immortality and knew Paradise.

In their lesser spheres many humbler rugby players have tasted the same ambrosia. All of us can picture and recall moments which were touched by the mysterious grace which can momentarily transfigure even Esher 3rd XV.

And there's fishing.

The dread moment comes in one's early or late thirties, when one is still stiff and sore on Saturday morning from the match on the previous Saturday afternoon, and one realises it is time to hang up one's boots. Some players feel that life thereafter has nothing to offer but decline: one has left Olympus for the long downhill march to the Underworld.

Not so! Apart from the abiding pleasures of a faithful tum, and the no longer entirely unmentionable and surprisingly lasting pleasures of the bed, there is the joy of passing on the pleasures of life to one's small children. There is, for those who have chosen luckily and wisely, the tremendous bonus of a job suited to their talents and interests, challenging, absorbing and helpful to one's community; so many go through the motions reluctantly for the sake of money, living only for and during their holidays. There are still games, a little slower and less ambitious, and there is music.

The Walter Mitty that lurks in all of us suspects that to be an Ashkenazy or a Barenboim must be the peak of human achievement and delight. We may never know the stunned hush and thunderous applause that sweeps across the crowded ranks of Europe's most sensitive and intelligent audiences; we may never dab an immaculate handkerchief to our temples as we bask in the sunshine of the adulation of millions, after our uniquely brilliant rendering of the last movement of the Emperor Concerto, but we can register tiny improvements in our own drawing room rendering of the easier classics and dream our dreams, and momentarily catch a hint of true musicality. And there is great music to raise our spirits at the touch of a button.

If there is time there may be a chance to try painting or some other form of creative art: it is all absorbing, utterly fascinating, always challenging and fiendishly difficult - yet infinitely rewarding, if one achieves even the most modest success.

And there is fishing.

Then retirement. This is supposed to be a time of weary resignation, when people feel useless and unloved. After the age of 60 the future can look frightening and energy is fading. Yet sheer delight is still there. At last we have time: time to stand and stare at the variety and beauty of nature. Time - and freedom from responsibility - to work at music and painting and writing, and to share these pleasures with family and friends. Time to travel.

36

And time to fish.

Finally, creaking old age, when physical activities are taken from you one by one. Old age full of joyful memories, in which the delights of music and painting and writing can accompany you with a little luck to the end or nearly the end of the road.

And there is fishing, with all its memories.

Always there is fishing. Gareth Edwards once said he would rather hook, play and land a good salmon than score a try for Wales. Fly fishing, especially, offers the full gamut of pleasure from extreme and wild excitement and even physical challenge to absorption in beautiful nature, from subtle skill to pure luck, from tense hope to glorious triumph. Always there is the breathless wait for that heart stopping moment when a big fish rises to take our fly.

Fishing combines so many other joys - the cooling music of the waters and the heat of the chase, gentle contemplation and desperate struggles, the song of birds and the quiet companionship of wild animals, the delight of skill and timing, the height of achievement and the depths of despair. In its train follow a host of absorbing arts and sciences, intimate knowledge of the times and seasons and of insect and water-side life, the delicate art of the fly tyer, the understanding and love of one's friends and enemies: the trout, the sea trout and the salmon. Above all the precious chance to be away from the hassle of human society and to re-establish harmony with nature in solitude.

How could life have been more fun?

One thing only I would change. There is no figure more sad than the old pavilion bore who haunts the scenes of his youthful successes when he is old and forgotten and fat, and has developed no other interest. I would therefore cultivate earlier the delights, which endure with the advancing years. If more games players started to enjoy painting or music or writing or nature study or fishing at an earlier age, they would do these things better and enjoy them more. Perhaps, most devoutly to be desired, they might even make their living through most of their lives doing what they like best.

Those who saw the TV interview of old Phil Drabble will have had a rare insight into what satisfaction a harmonious life can bring. It may be good to be Prime Minister, but it may possibly be more important to bring up wild creatures on the bottle and to be rewarded when a white fawn rushes from the woods to greet you and to kiss you with warm and loving enthusiasm on both cheeks!

Past Overs

School cricket has been a sad casualty of the Age of Haste. Just as 'fast food' has replaced roast beef and Yorkshire pudding, the pressures of modern life are driving out the graceful and timeless game, and replacing it with various shortened versions of the 'pyjama game'.

Educationists can no longer defend cricket as it was played at schools like Tonbridge in the days of Alan Knott and Colin Cowdrey. Every boy played for 10 hours a week, bar a few specially licensed and totally unco-ordinated eccentrics. Anyone with a grain of potential played for 15 hours or more. Potential scientists, artists, poets and musicians scored ducks and dropped catches in blue-fingered misery - or so half of our bilious middle-aged auto-biographers tell us.

It was all, they say, a part of the ridiculous 'games blood' élitism, which gave precedence and enjoyment to athletes at the expense of academic progress, and which brought unhappiness and boredom to the majority.

Others, not always athletes, paint a different picture. Old-fashioned cricket was not necessarily highly athletic. It cast a spell over many who were indifferent players, or were merely spectators. There were days - occasionally weeks - when to be white flannelled on a dreamy English cricket field was a leisured foretaste of heaven. The artists and poets made daisy chains in the deep, as they watched swallows flicker low over the sun-drenched grass. The musicians listened entranced to the burbling of willow warblers and blackcaps as the elm tree shadows lengthened. Unathletic spectators lay on the grass, blissfully hypnotised by the rhythmic movements of the white players on golden afternoons and the satisfying resonance of well-timed strokes.

Moreover, it should not be forgotten that school cricket has moments of excitement unequalled at Lord's, the Oval or Trent Bridge. When Willie Athill, aged 12, got 10 wickets for, I believe, less than one run each, he achieved something that even the great Tony Lock failed to emulate.

These things are possible at junior level because of a combination of 'flexible umpiring' and the psychological vulnerability of the young. If a team of 12-year-olds is convinced (and how easily that is done!) that they are facing a demon bowler enjoying a unique run of form, they will get themselves out. Willie was a great guy, but he struck little terror in the batsmen's hearts in later years. At the time, however, it was sheer drama.

Every afternoon a dozen games were in progress at every school. Strange things happened that passed unnoticed in *Wisden*. One Norfolk pupil suffered mild attacks of *petit mal*. His co-pupils recognised the nature of his attacks and knew what to do, treating him calmly and kindly. One day he was opening the batting. He struck a four, reeled round a couple of times, waving his bat, and fell to the ground. The wicket-keeper and first slip held his gloved hands and waited quietly for his recovery, which took only a few seconds. He stood up and took guard again. 'Feel OK, Rodney?' asked the umpire. 'Fine, thanks!'

He hit the next ball for another four.

Umpiring was good at the top, but wobbled by the time you got to Juniors C. At best it wobbled through ignorance, rather than unfairness. Below Colts, to be struck anywhere on the pads portended the end of your innings. The intricacies of the lbw law were beyond lower forms and their teachers.

On the other hand, there were head teacher umpires, especially in prep schools, whose unscrupulous bias in favour of their own schools was not excused by ignorance. I remember one such taking over as umpire in a crisis. From square leg he noted with satisfaction that the opposition's star batsman had allowed himself to be struck on the pad. The bowler, knowing it was 2 ft outside the leg stump, didn't appeal. The head was no whit deterred. Although he knew it was the decision of the very young teacher at the bowler's end, he called out from square leg: 'Did I hear you appeal, James? Ah ... I thought so!' And he shamelessly raised his index finger, brooking no argument.

Incidents came thick and fast. A hundred was scored by one batsman in 20 minutes, because the groundsman had prepared a square with a 30 yard leg-side boundary. Every half-holiday several matches would be played simultaneously on a vast field without defined boundaries between the different games. The confusion caused bizarre umpiring problems. Fielder in match A suddenly woke up and caught a massive hit from match B in front of the nose of a pursuing fielder from that match. What should the decision be?

Conscript cricket had to go. The cynical head-master who said it was 'like homosexuality, best practised in private between consenting adults' reflected the mood of the times. Middle-distance runners,swimmers, tennis players, gymnasts, artists and musicians are now rightly released to follow their bent. The cricketers have been pruned to a small number of promising enthusiasts playing for a much reduced time. It is no longer a leisured world, and the leisured classes are disappearing. The old form of cricket may linger in a few public schools, together with the cane and Greek, but it is changing even there.

It is much better than no cricket at all: but spare a tear for the elegance of the peaceful game that was a part of an Olde England some of us loved.

Swinging Through Life

'Their memorial a thousand lost golf balls!' Thus T. S. Eliot ironically castigated Homo Suburbia in general, and the futility of golf in particular.

Poets and intellectuals are seldom sympathetic to games players. Viewed from the supercilious peaks of Parnassus, golf vies with bridge for the reputation of the greatest time-waster of the middle classes: interminable, exclusive, expensive, and accompanied by recriminatory and protracted post-mortems.

Although lacking the judgment and mental alertness for the one, and the temperamental and physical control for the other, I do not share this view; I love both, especially golf.

If you have been a serious and competitive games player, you need one game in which you have no ambitions. Golf is ideal.

At first sight it seems ridiculously undemanding. It needs no great physique or courage. No opponent puts the ball out of reach, or thumps it straight at your midriff from a few feet away, as in squash or tennis. No one is licensed to knock you to the ground or bash all the wind from your body as in rugby. All you have to do is hit an innocent, motionless and conspicuous ball off a small peg of adjustable height.

If you hit it fairly straight and firmly, though without violence, up the fairway, within one, two, or at worst three strokes, you will find yourself on a lawn as smooth as a billiard table (if not quite as true). You then have to tap your little ball gently into a broad and receptive hole.

Moreover, if you miss the first time, but succeed at second attempt, you are still considered a useful player. How can grown men indulge in such an easy pastime? And how can some of them not only fail to sink the ball on the green in two shots, but hit it into gorse bushes and sand pits, taking three, four or even five strokes to reach the green?

At 17, I found out. My father took me to St Andrew's for a three-week holiday playing two rounds a day. I was a strong, ignorant lad; my first drive went 270 yards straight down the middle. It was a sunny day, there was a following wind, the gorse was in bloom, the larks were singing and all the violins in heaven and earth played.

My second led to a rather closer look at the blooming gorse. Advice was given, and I started to think.

I sliced, and concentrated, as instructed, on swinging from in to out. I hooked, and concentrated on the angle of my club face. I concentrated on my grip, and I topped the ball. The supple ease of my youthful swing disappeared for ever beneath a heap of complexes, as I wondered about my left shoulder, tried to feel my left hand leading, pondered about the cocking of my wrists, calculated the position of my feet, and finally degenerated into a disharmonious mass of jarring muscles and joints.

I never hit another good drive, and have been trying to recover enough simplicity to re-enter the Garden of Eden ever since. When, on the last day, I achieved the almost impossible by doing an air shot with my putter on the admittedly vast 18th green, I knew I would never be any good. But I loved it...Why?

Golf is especially fun if you are erratic and past your physical prime. At what other sport can you hope to improve not merely at 40, but at 50 and 60? At what other sport can a second-rate amateur suddenly play a hole like the Open champion, and the Open champion suddenly miss a three-foot putt? Hope never dies.

If most of your shots are bad, a moderate one gives pleasure, and the occasional fluked master-stroke brings wild delight: a sweetly hit iron has a tingling feeling about it, like timing a late cut. How much happier the rabbit who unexpectedly gets a par four than the professional who strays from dull perfection through mental exhaustion and misses his usual birdie at the same hole! You play in beautiful places at your own pace, away from income tax returns, washing up and television. You hate nothing and nobody except one small ball.

Golfing opponents, contrary to their reputation for snootiness, are kind and tolerant. In this they are helped by the certainty of victory, and the enduring pleasure, which close friends may conceal but never conquer, of watching an opponent's ball topple gently into bunker after bunker.

Golf is also a microcosm of life. Nothing takes so much humility. In no other game must the Old Adam within be so controlled: the more tense your determination, the more ferocious the power you apply, the more certain the retribution.

The borderline between cheating and gamesmanship is tenous. When my brother selected his club on the short 11th at Sheringham, facing a stiffish wind, he said: 'This looks just about a number seven!' He landed the ball near the middle of the green, holding his follow through as if for the photographers - long enough to allow me to glance at the bottom of the club to confirm my suspicion that it was a number five and not a number seven. All is fair in family golf, but it was near enough to cheating to justify well chosen reprisals.

Nevertheless, when the golfers and the poets are weighed in the great final scales, the niblick may be held to have done less harm than the pen, and even Eliot might well have gained in humility and understanding from a quick round or two.

41

Special Magic

The evening rise is widely celebrated in angling literature. When the elusive British summer allows us brief glimpses of flaming June, or occasional hot, still nights in July and August, the two hours before dusk can produce great fishing in magical surroundings.

Yet dawn is better. After their night's rest, the trout are hungrier, and the riverside has recovered something of the freshness of spring. The lochs are alive with animals and birds, before the daily intrusion of the human world drives them back to the undergrowth, or to their nests and holes. The trout too seem less suspicious, as though they expect no trouble at such a peaceful hour.

In the 1960s and '70s I used to escape on many summer mornings at 5.30 or 6 a.m. to put in an hour and a half of fishing on the little Glaven river in Norfolk, before the start of the day's work. On return I would tear off my waders, and hurry to change and to eliminate the smell of fish, before the first boys queued up outside my study at eight o'clock with their strange assortment of problems. It was a spiritual and physical refreshment to fortify anyone against the dustiest of days.

For some reason - old age, idleness or some such excuse - I have not done this so much in retirement. If one has the whole day at one's disposal, one is not obliged to squeeze fishing into the hours before 8 am or after 8 pm. The special magic of dawn can be forgotten.

But special magic it is, as I was reminded early this summer. After a fairly unsuccessful midday sortie, and eschewing the evening rise for fear too many other anglers, released from their work, would have the same idea, I decided to return at dawn.

There was not another car on the road, not a breath of wind, not a cloud in the sky, not a soul by the water. The sun was already warming my shoulders as I pulled on my waders. Yet the air was fresh. The green leaves were dew-washed and jewel bright. The sedge warblers, blackcaps and whitethroats were singing as though they were newly arrived and free of family cares.

I put up my rod by the Glandford ford. The picturesque little footbridge, the lovely old mill house and the flint church were reflected in a mill pool without a ripple - except for those caused by a pair of swans with their cygnets, and a host of ducklings. As I stood under the trees on the corner pool above the bridge, a kingfisher flashed by with the sun full on its ultramarine and turquoise back, and the first two trout broke the surface, rising quietly and purposefully.

I caught one, first cast. Then I nearly trod on a mallard's nest, and the mother duck insisted on trailing her 'broken wing' upstream for 100 yds, slapping the water like a drunken oarsman and disturbing every trout in the small stream for the next three pools.

I progressed slowly up the river to the point where the Glaven narrows to a mere 5ft or 6ft between banks of weeds and reeds about head high; towards the top of the beat there are overhanging trees. By 6.30 there was a slight breeze against, and to land a fly near a rising trout was quite a challenge. Nevertheless I had collected breakfast for my wife and for me.

Walking back to the car down a bank liberally sprinkled with campion, forget-me-nots and yellow flags, it was hard to believe that this was overpopulated England, threatened by the doom of pollution in all its forms. I drove back along still-empty roads to breakfast in a secluded garden, with walls of pink brick and flint, all sunshine and roses. What a privilege in a country which can still be as kind and beautiful as any in the world.

I only hope our great grandchildren will be as lucky.

The Importance of Playing Games Badly

About four years ago, Britain discovered 60 per cent of its 16 year olds took no organised exercise whatever. Exeter University research indicated that, even before that age, most school pupils took no more exercise than the equivalent of a two mile walk every week; not enough to prepare their hearts adequately for adult life.

Things have improved, but not much. The Seventies and Eighties movement against team games has still damaged their status in many schools. The core curriculum left little time for 'fringe' activities, and a lot of schools found it impossible to fit in two periods of P.E. per week and abandoned games outside classroom hours.

To compensate, clubs and leisure centres tried to recruit promising young athletes, with some success. The result has been a fast-growing gap between a gifted, highly competitive minority, playing, if they were big, fast, strong and dedicated, for large sums of money, and a majority who sit in armchairs eating chocolates and watching the minority perform for their entertainment. It does not do much for their fitness. There was a letter to *The Times* in March from a

43

Leeds University student saying that over 100 rugby enthusiasts had been denied a game because there were only fixtures and organisations for our 'top' squad.

The professionals are concerned only with success in sports and games which have grown increasingly violent. There is little sense of fun and adventure, not much elegance or cunning. Winners are the youngest, strongest, most ruthless and most scientifically prepared. Regional and national prestige is ridiculously much at stake and the press and the spectators put so much pressure on the players that avoidance of defeat has come to justify any tactics. It is now common and understandable to see losers weeping and victors gloating.

There are still a few brave amateurs, who play for enjoyment: village cricketers, rustic rugby clubs, cheerful hockey teams, occasional footballers. In most sports they are, unfortunately, dwindling. Nobody can take his or her career seriously and expect to excel in any sport 'on the side'. Children watch sport on television, despair of ever succeeding among the giant top players and help themselves to another chocolate. If you weigh only 12 stone, however fit and strong you may be, you cannot contemplate being a rugby forward. If you cannot do 100m in under 12 seconds, there is no chance of your becoming a three quarter.

If you want to play tennis seriously, you might as well give up if you have not the basic technique and strength to thump a ball accurately at over 100 miles an hour. If you want to be a cricketer, you must at least have the quickness of reflexes to defend yourself against deadly missiles hurled by large aggressive men of well over 6ft.

Violence has become so much a part of team games that a referee cannot bring himself to send off a forward who launches four punches against the opposition in an international match. In squash, as in tennis, delicacy is swept off the court by power, percentage and pressure. The result has been that adults who wish to keep fit have increasingly turned to non-competitive activities - aerobics, jogging, rambling, cycling or dancing.

What is needed, if all competitive sport is not to be grimly serious and dominated by sheer size and power, is a return to the enjoyment of playing badly. Not deliberately badly, of course - if people do not want to win, they make games boring. One should want to triumph, whether in tiddlywinks, happy families, or Monopoly. But everyone should be able to enjoy the exercise, comradeship and fun at his or her own level, at school and afterwards.

There should be a return to genuinely amateur sport for people who cannot afford more than three or four hours a week.

How often matches between top teams are dull. Every player knows every weakness of the opposition, every possibility of a mistake is eliminated. When such pressures have gone, enterprise, risk and fun can return. There should be tournaments in which the players laugh on the field of play, and genuinely congratulate each other. If necessary, they should play to different rules - which ensure skill and cunning can play as much of a part as sheer power. Certainly there should be more chances for people of similar size and physique to enjoy competitions among themselves in school and afterwards - in rugby, hockey, football, and in athletics, especially in events like the shot, the discus and the hammer. Games can be a joy to anyone if there is a chance for the rapier to overcome the bludgeon.

At school and in adult life we should not be forced to choose between being cannon fodder for giants and being mere spectators.

Buttercups and Bulls

You will have heard of the Lune: plenty of brown trout, good night fishing for sea trout and some fair sized salmon. Its dramatic rock pools in the middle reaches and its bubbling power lower down make it unique among Northern English rivers. At the great swirling Waters' Meet pool, it divides in two, near where the borders of Yorkshire, Lancashire and Westmorland used to fuse. The more southerly branch, often carrying the greater weight of water, is the River Rawthey. You are much less likely to have heard of the Rawthey, perhaps because it figures less prominently in the salmon and sea trout records. It winds its way past Sedbergh up to Baugh Fell and to Wild Boar Fell.

If you can catch the Rawthey on a sunny week at the end of May or at the beginning of June, it can be as varied and beautiful a river as any in Britain. It gave my father hours of blissful escape, I was never happier than on its banks, my nephews learned there, and I hope it will not be long before my grandsons follow suit. Not all of our apprenticeships were legal. One relative used to catch up on his sleep during classes at Sedbergh school after all night expeditions - more thrilling than fruitful - spearing salmon. He is now Doing Well...

From the Waters' Meet with the Lune, full of good fish, but hard to cover because of cross currents and backwaters, there is ideal trout water all the way to Lord's Dub: a great, deep slab-rocked pool, into which the turbulent water is funnelled through hurtling, narrow channels. It was in a not very good pool below this that I once took my wife down to show her how to cast. On my first demonstration cast, I hooked and landed a trout of 1lb 14oz: a big one for those parts. It is not the sort of thing which often happens, although my brother caught a seven pound salmon on trout tackle nearby. There is a good high summer evening rise along the very edge of the deeper shore of the pools on the bends a little downstream from there. Above Lord's Dub, between Jackdaw Bridge and the confluence of the Rawthey and the little river Dee, there are rocky runs from 2 to 3 feet deep. At the right time, trout are there for the taking from the slower eddies behind the larger rocks. An upstream wet fly (Partridge and Orange or Snipe and Purple) fished on a short line is most effective. A stealthy angle can induce them to rise, especially if the water is a little coloured, within a rod's length.

The Dee leads up to the pretty village of Dent: plenty of trout, but rather smaller. The Rawthey itself, as it nears Sedbergh, passes through woods with bluebells and wild garlic, alternating with buttercup and dandelion meadows of unequalled lushness. There is no shortage of water: I remember playing mud-soaked rugby during a first week of October in which there were twelve inches of rain. It was in one of these idyllic meadows that, encumbered with waders, net and rod, on a very hot day, I was charged by a huge brown bull. After I had vaulted the dry stone wall, with my lead cut down to a mere five yards, I thanked God for the sound construction, which thwarted the bull's obvious desire to knock the wall down and gore me as I paused to pick up the rod and net I'd hurled over the wall ahead of me.

Near Sedbergh itself, the fells each side grow higher: the treeless, glistening ochraceous mountains of Winder, Higher Winder and the Calf dominate the well treed Rawthey valley. Milthrop Bridge is only a few hundred yards from the school itself. My sister-in-law, leaning over that bridge, once bet me £5 that I wouldn't wade across the river in spate. It was a lot of money in those days, and I was wearing the kilt. I won the £5, and was soaked to the armpits. From that same parapet, Sedbergh boys would dangle worms - or wire nooses - for trout or eels and, on gala days, a salmon.

Above Sedbergh the woods make the fishing difficult. It was there and in the Clough that a boy called Kelsall was King. The tiny Clough is a tributary leading to the caves near Danny Bridge by a succession of pools and minor waterfalls. Kelsall's highly skilled spinning produced some lovely baskets of considerable trout from that narrow and tricky stream. He later, very properly, became Fisheries Officer for Lake Victoria...

Four miles upstream from Sedbergh, the river emerges from the woods near the Cross Keys Hotel, no wider than a big burn. There is a splendid view of Cautley crags, split by the long white plume of Cautley Spout: the haunt of ravens and of buzzards, and formerly of peregrines. After long treks across the fells or up the river, the Cross Keys offered a taste of Heaven. Ham as thick as

46

your hand, and eggs, scones, cream and strawberry jam. Oh! And Vimto, red and sticky, but like champagne when we were heavy-legged and facing a long return journey.

The buttercup meadows have given way to heather by the time the river turns up the bleak flanks of Baugh Fell, but it is still rocky rather than peaty. Half pounders, that far up, are rare, but the fishing easy.

As a boy I caught few fish: too much downstream fishing, too long flogging the wrong parts of the river, the wrong time, too much dependent on August holidays. Returning years later, I did much better. I believe it would respond better still to Tweedside dry fly techniques, though they are unfashionable in Cumbria.

For boys it provided an abundance of freedom, high adventure and un-forgettable beauty, which taught us as much as the excellent teaching.

It still does.

In Praise of Schubert

When the B.B.C. decides to do something worthwhile, it does it well. Anniversary programmes are often a bore, but this year their efforts with Schubert have been marvellous.

I'm biased - something to do with my German grandmother, no doubt. I get uncomfortable shivers at Wagnerian music, and reach surreptitiously for my handkerchief at Schumann. A corner of me is Scottish enough to be ashamed of that, but no one need conceal unashamed delight, joy and tears, when he hears Schubert, because it is music of transparent genuineness and goodness.

Why has he been so neglected compared with Beethoven or Bach? It cannot be that we all prefer the vast and monumental and powerful to the more brief and evanescent beauties of pure lyricism. In a cynical and sophisticated age, Schubert may seem almost naïvely emotional. Apart from two great symphonies, he provides little for the concert and opera repertoires of contemporary fashion. Vast concert halls and the mass audiences are not for him; above all composers he is intimate. His Lieder are for artists who can establish a close relationship with each member of a small audience. They do not require great over-trained voices so much as romantics of the profoundest understanding and delicacy.

47

That is why Wilfred Brown, for instance, was, to those privileged to hear and understand him, more profoundly moving in a drawing room recital than Dietrich Fischer Dieskau. Schubert composed to entangle his friends, performers and audience in a community of joy and sorrow in a manner that thrived on physical nearness. Paradoxically, television is a most effective vehicle for him. The magic box that makes all things small is powerless to reduce Schubert - it just brings him home to us in an intimate way.

Impromptus, sonatas, moments musical, trios, the schöne Müllerin and the Winterreise - all marvellous. The height of lyricism was reached, however, in the Trout Quintet. It may not have the heartbreaking profundity of some of the Winterreise songs, or the mystery and drama of Erlkönig, but it has magic. However much the Trout theme has been done to death by the vulgarity of incurably English performers unaware of the crudity of their acts of murder, this performance of the Quintet by young and gifted soloists, recorded from rehearsal to ultimate perfection was sheer joy...well on second thoughts, not perfection. Performances of Schubert should never be perfect. Franz was too spontaneous and human, and his music calls for youth and abandon, even exaggeration. Despair, ebullience, bitterness, sweetness and exhilaration can be driven out by perfection, or cramped by over intelligent good taste.

What wonderful viewing that great Quintet provided. Jacqueline du Prés at her best making her 'cello bound and quiver with her own joy. Zukerman apparently as far beyond any technical limitations as if he had been playing his normal first violin role. Opposite him the infinitely expressive and happy face of the violinist Perlman from much the same musical background as himself, responding to and conveying the tiniest whispers of mood-and-tempo-change with a similarity of musical interpretation and temperament which had to be seen to be believed. The bass player, Zubin Mehta, more often thought of as a conductor, seemed to be caught up into and held in this mysterious unity, as though in a trance.

This unity necessarily owed as much to the pianist as to anybody. In the Trout the piano often provides the constant movement of the water in which the other instruments sparkle and flash and ripple and tumble in turn. The pianist Daniel Barenboim, seemed electrically aware of what everyone was doing, the ideal accompanist, never obtruding, always precise, always providing the framework on which the others could embroider, but himself embroidering and embellishing with the rest as the roles exchanged.

Programme music that imitates cuckoos or thunder, and tells stories can be (forgive me, Beethoven) irritating. But the Trout Quintet never labours its descriptiveness. It is pure, sunlit water music, the essence of spring by the brookside. The phrases dart and trill, ebb and flow in interweaving liquid

48

patterns: they are like eddies and swirls and bubbles, sparkling and dazzling their rhythmic way over a gleaming mosaic of pebbles. The cameras did it all justice; hands and arms, smiling lips and raised eyebrows, bows and keys performed a ballet; melodies and accompaniments shuttled back and forth as faces were utterly lost in the joy of recreation.

Is there anything more thrilling in music than the movement in which, towards the end, the 'cello and the bass take up the central melody slowly and peacefully against this restless onward drive of the rippling piano? Schubert understood water music from the dance of the mill wheels to the ruffling of a still pool by the first chill breeze of evening. No angler could listen to him without a thrill of recognition.

In his choice of poems to set to music Schubert had instinctive good taste. The greatest and best poems of his time sprang to music in his mind. To this good taste there was, apparently, one exception. The words of Wilhelm Müller's schöne Müllerin and Winterreise, to which Schubert wrote so many of his most beautiful melodies and accompaniments, have seemed, to many critics, sentimental, commonplace and full of cliché. I believe they miss the point.

The one great quality which lay slumbering in Müller's over-simple verse, waiting for Schubert's touch to awaken it, was the agonised, nostalgic, bitter sweet, tragic passion for all the evanescent pleasures of life of a young man doomed to an early death.

This at once struck the deepest chord of recognition in Schubert, in whose hands the mood came alive and gained immortality. And because we are all the prisoners of a dying animal, Schubert and Müller brought the human condition home to us with a heightened force and sincerity that has never been excelled. It is this which will ensure that to sentimental amateurs like myself (who will always be in the majority), Schubert will survive all the changes of taste and fashion and keep the very special place he deserves.

The Treasures of Scotland

For some incomprehensible reason there has, in this catalogue of pleasures, been hardly a mention of the activity which has given me the most constant delight of all: fishing in Scotland.

No disrespect to fishing in Norfolk or Yorkshire; it has all been a joy, but in Scotland it is special. Every year from the age of 6 to 19 I spent summer and/or Easter holidays trout fishing in the North - and whenever possible since.

Although the fishing was often good, it is the staggering variety of beauty which is my abiding memory. Scotland has an unbelievable amount of delightful water scenery. It looks a small country on the map, yet it has a longer coastline than all Europe from St Petersburg round to the Dardanelles. The myriad islands, the sea lochs and lochans provide an inexhaustible kaleidoscope of loveliness.

Yes, I know...it rains! I used to leave my wife with two or more small children in a caravan or a tent playing snakes and ladders while I caught sea trout. One day we returned from a walk to find a sad-eyed and shaggy Highland bullock with 5 feet of canvas from the tent's roof dangling from its mouth. I was justly sentenced to serve 20 summers in the south of France.

The Highland weather is, however, miraculously changeable. If there are heavy clouds now, the sky will be cærulean blue tomorrow or this afternoon. Gales blow up within hours or minutes, only to give way just as quickly to complete stillness. There may be Mediterranean sun at the bottom of the glen, a storm at the top. Rainbows - even double or treble rainbows - are common. People talk of the light which is the glory of Greece, Italy or India. In Scotland there is every kind of light.

'Before you die,' they say, 'you must see the Grand Canyon, Niagara, the snows of Kilimanjaro, 150 miles from Darjeeling, touched by the pink light of morning, the Taj Mahal by moonlight.' True, but when you've been astonished by the vastness, the majesting power, the glory and the magic, that's it! If you lived with any of them the impression would fade. In Scotland, the variety of the light, the landscapes and the seasons is such that you couldn't exhaust or indeed witness all its beauty in three or four lifetimes. Canada's lakes and waterways are magnificent, but they are often very much the same for hundreds of miles.

Scotland's crowning glory must be the views of Eigg, Muck, Rhum and the Cuillins viewed from Sanna or Morar or from any of the high peaks of the western mainland. The changeable weather and the rain-washed skies produce a turquoise back cloth, on which the setting sun paints amazing cloud patterns in crimson and vermilion, deep purple, indigo and flame. The silhouettes of the islands, jagged, sensuous and surreal seem suspended between the spectacular skies and their mirror image in the sea. The evening performance may be often repeated, but it is never the same for 5 minutes. No wonder Scottish artists have had the decent humility not to attempt to paint these sunsets, or hide their efforts in shame if they do.

Other Hebridean islands or sea lochs have their own variations on this theme, and every one of Scotland's thousands of waters has its own character and magic: each has a wealth of history and legend entwined with the settings and the clans which live nearby. The pass of Brander, where the river Awe links the sea and the loch below Ben Cruachan, is deep, black and menacing. The Tweed at Scott's view winds its way between wooded slopes, carpeted with primroses and daffodils beneath the violet Eildon Hills: it can smile, or be fierce, treacherous and grim, hurling dead sheep and uprooted trees along its irresistible flood waters. There are countless burns, each with its hidden waterfalls and secret, deep and gin-clear pools, framed in a tartan of scarlet rowans, purple heather, lime green moss and silver birches. The Spey itself is an exuberant overgrown burn swirling its way through a rich valley between colourful moors and the stark Cairngorms. October adds siennas and rusts to the riot of colours.

Every loch and river has its own naiads and dryads, birds and animals which seem to incorporate the spirit of their homes. Curlews haunt a favourite hill loch in the Borders. Surely their ecstatic yet tragic trilling is the most beautiful of all bird songs. Another, in the Highlands, wilder and more spectral, echoes to the uncanny wailing of divers. The Don in springtime is surrounded by black and white flocks of lapwings and oystercatchers, shrilling and piping against the rich ochres of the nearby ploughed fields. Above all these waters are shaped by the dozens of mountains with unforgettable, improbable shapes and names remembered and treasured by every Scot: Schiehallion, Slioch, Ben Laoighal, Cruachan, Sgurr-nan-Gillean, Quinag, Stac Poly or the 'inaccessible pinnacle'.

My father wisely introduced them to me and fed my dreams and imagination by introducing new enchantments every year. At the age of seven, I watched him by moonlight, playing and catching three big sea trout on the black and silver mill pool at Rodel on the Isle of Harris. At the age of eight it was Ardnamurchan and Loch Mudle, where I fought and lost a salmon on my 7 foot rod - and wept.

Then it was Loch Awe with its huge fish and bizarre legends. At Port-sonachan there was a cast of a 53 lb salmon caught on 3 x gut and a light trout rod. Last century a brown trout of 39 lbs was caught, still nearly twice the size of the official British record. A black monster lurks in Loch Awe, feeding only on virgins. This is Campbell country and I fear it may have gone hungry. Later my father took me to Sutherland, where no man can hope to fish even a quarter of the lochs available, the glorious Applecross and Loch Maree, Scotland's highest village - Tomintoul - and the home of our MacGregor ancestors on Speyside.

We went for three years to the Don in the first week after the snow cleared from the water, never failing to catch trout of over 3 lbs in that wonderful river. In 1935 it cost (is it possible?) £6 a week for both of us with separate rooms, a drawing room with a grand piano, a 9-hole golf course and 3 miles of prime Don fishing! In later years my mother's house near St Boswell's gave me regular access to the Tweed, and a dear old friend has introduced me to the variety and beauty of the Alness.

In no people is the love of their landscape more deeply engrained than in the Scots. Their millions of exiles will learn to appreciate the glories of Kashmir, Kenya, New Zealand or the Rockies; but their highest praise is: 'Ay! It fair puts me in mind of...'

It may be irritating, but it is true. When God was doing the preliminary sketches for the great wonders of the world, he tried them out in full freshness and brightest colours in Scotland. When we Scots come to the final review of our lives, our crimes and our good deeds will alike give way to our memories of our homeland's loveliest land and waterscapes which will file past our eyes as a foretaste of Paradise.

Norfolk Life

The Secret Trout

Even non-fishermen know that giant pike have been caught in Hickling and that the Broads have been a centre for bream, roach, perch and tench for centuries. They may even have heard that zander are being caught in the Ouse. But Norfolk does not figure greatly in the legend and literature of trout fishing.

This must be due to the shrewd caution of the Norfolk character; for the trout fishing is certainly there. Norfolk countrymen have chosen to enjoy their own trout, in discreet seclusion from tourists and outsiders, and to avoid boastful propaganda outside the county.

They are in a minority. Truth does not figure strongly in the vast and readable literature of trout fishing. Visitors attracted to Ireland by the angling blarney tend to find that great catches of fish over three pounds were made in the previous week. When they have left, rumours reach them of even better catches the week after; but it is a case of Guinness yesterday and Guinness tomorrow, never Guinness today.

You don't need to be an expert to have read of the glories of Test and Windrush, Dove and Derwent, Eden and Lune. Scotland has a literature of its own. Welshmen, Devonians and Yorkshire Dalesmen advertise their rivers with a gusto quite unjustified by the size of their fish. Yet if you mention Norfolk trout in those parts of Britain, eyebrows shoot up: 'You mean gravel pits?' they ask.

There are indeed excellent gravel pits and reservoirs which provide first-rate still water fishing, but it is the rivers of Norfolk which are its secret glory. Most of them are owned by Norfolk farmers or syndicates; most are off the beaten track. If you question them, wise Norfolk eyes crinkle defensively, and vague references are made to there having been some trout some years ago, but not many nowadays.

Long may it remain so. Syndicates look after their stretches sensibly and unostentatiously, and subscriptions, by southern standards, are not expensive. The river board keeps a close eye on any increase in pollution and does its best to strike the difficult balance between the farmers' need to drain their riverside fields and avoid flooding, the anglers' need to avoid over-dredging and pollution, and the wildlife enthusiasts' desire to preserve meadow and marshland.

On the Bure, the Wensum, the Wissey, the Nar, the Glaven and (at least potentially) the Stiffkey, there is trout fishing which is all that the heart could desire. Large parts of them are genuine chalk streams. There are pools which repeatedly produce specimen trout of over five pounds; there are upper reaches no more than two or three yards wide, overgrown by trees and with tangles of head-high weeds and brambles defending the approaches, full of small trout and extremely difficult to fish. There are fast, pebble-bottomed, gin-clear streams, as swift as Highland burns; there are broad sweeping pools with powerful currents at the head., backwaters with flotillas of Duns where big fish lurk among tree roots; there are long and varied stretches where the depth shelves between two and five feet, and where the bottom changes between firm footing and treacherous glutinous mud.

There are corkscrewing reaches where the varied pace of the stream drives a channel between wavy weed banks, which makes it hair-raisingly difficult to play even a pound trout. The banks can be safe and treeless, wooded, tangled, high or low. Always they are enchanting places to spend an afternoon in May, surrounded by buttercup meadows and bluebell copses, while the anorak between your shoulder blades warms to the new season sun.

There are still lots of kingfishers and a few sandpipers. Sedge warblers and blackcaps are singing all around; at every bend there is a moorhen's nest miraculously preserved from being swept away. There are plenty of herons to take advantage of the lack of cover for trout after too extensive dredging; some of the lower reaches have banks which are still crumbling from the attention of coypu. Two years ago a genuinely wild family of otters bred successfully not far from my home.

It would not be right, even in an East Anglian paper, to analyse the best places or their ownership. There is a beat on one river where I once caught eight trout of over a pound in a couple of hours; it looked like the Test, and fished like it.

54

I was lucky enough to be a guest on a different river last year. There was a thunderstorm; I fell in, I tore my trousers on barbed wire, scratched my leg on brambles and was stung by nettles. Yet I have never fished better or enjoyed myself more, catching and returning to the water nearly every trout which rose ....and there were plenty.

That is the peculiar attraction of Norfolk trout fishing. There is something repulsively over-civilised about the excessively well-tended southern chalk streams. Branches which might ensnare your back cast are trimmed, the best lies are marked by well knelt-on, weed-clear patches on the banks, barbed wire fences are rendered innocuous by sacking. Stiles and plank bridges are kept in repair and do not crumble beneath your weight. Even the trout have some of the corpulent sleepiness of post-prandial executives.

Personally I would rather struggle with the unkempt wilderness of Norfolk streams and fight for a fit and streamlined three-quarter pounder than have it all laid on for a fat domesticated fish of twice the size. But, with any luck, you can have your cake and eat it. There are few seasons in which trout between five and ten pounds are not caught somewhere in Norfolk.

Tall Tales

Although one must have some of those marvellous modern natural history reference books to check facts, speculation and tall stories are more fun. That is why I prefer to talk to old Norfolk countrymen, or to read the old bird books.

Some years ago, plagued by moles, I turned to my vintage Norfolk gardener for advice. He told me that if I sank a bottle in a shallow mole tunnel up to the neck, I would be rid of the moles the next day. The neck of the bottle must be left protruding so that the wind would set up a musical hum of such penetrating vibrations that the mole, ultra-sensitive to any movements, if it didn't die of shock, would make its escape, half-crazed, to a neighbour's bottleless garden. I ranked this bit of advice with the gamekeeper's tale that he used to catch rabbits in his youth by placing a brick across a rabbit run, sprinkling it with pepper and waiting for the rabbit to bust its brains out by sneezing. Charlie, however, insisted with such eloquence that I finally consented to half bury an empty bottle of Burgundy under his instructions. My site inspection early next morning revealed a mole lying dead on the grass beside the bottle. A brief post mortem established the fact that it had been killed by a mole trap rather than by vibrational brain storm....

Truth is not always so easily disentangled from Norfolk legend, with its basis of earthy knowledge embroidered with zest and humour. I know of one

Norfolk mole catcher who saves himself the bother of digging or trapping by listening, watching, and listening again in order to shoot moles unerringly in their shallow underground runs.

Any Norfolk countryman of middle age or over will have been brought up on tall stories: rustic Munchausens with their feet more or less on the ground and a genuine knowledge of nature, mingling truth and fiction in arbitrary proportions. I have been told how rabbits used to be driven from their burrows by sending crabs down sideways with little candles stuck on the top of their shells. I have heard how quantities of song birds were lured to lime twigs by imitating the call of the hated long-eared owl. Small birds cannot resist mobbing the owl, and scores were caught.

Before Darwin spoiled it all with a cold shower of close observation, bird books were full of intriguing secondhand stories passed on in good faith. Stanley, Bishop of Norwich, the Revd F.O.Morris, even on occasion the sharp-eyed Gilbert White, wrote about nature in a way which constantly makes us wonder where truth ends and credulity, hearsay or superstition take its place.

It was a blend of Christian tradition and lack of clear observation that led sailors to believe that the pelican, if it had not found enough fish, would pierce its own heart and feed it to its young - a symbol of Christian sacrifice. The distant sight of the young burying their heads in the deep recesses of that wide open beak, pulling out bloody remnants of fish, must have looked very like noble suicide.

There were 'authenticated cases' of an eagle carrying off a child both in Orkney and in Skye: both were subsequently rescued. A captive eagle in Vienna lived in a cage for 104 years. Another golden eagle was killed by a mastiff, but the dog itself died of its wounds shortly afterwards.

Barn owls love music, tawny owls have never been seen drinking, little owls drink large quantities every night. In 1849 at Bridlington, a honey buzzard flapped and beat its wings against a householder's bedroom window until he opened it and caught the bird by hand.

Every year 22,600 gannets used to be eaten by the inhabitants of St Kilda. The Bishop of Capri used to get 20,000 francs a year from the 150,000 quails which were killed annually as they landed exhausted on his island after migration. Herons, after swallowing live eels, are compelled to 'place their rumps against hillocks or stones to prevent the fish from getting out again'.

And to cap it all, a Red Indian tribe has so perfected a call to attract the American eagle that they only have to stand still with their hunting knives pointing straight up above their heads for the eagles to stoop down and impale themselves......Take your pick.

Red Deer, Squirrels and a Lost Sheep

There's no better time for seeing animals than dawn and dusk in spring and autumn. East Anglia has many surprises for those who are out and about at such times and keep their eyes alert.

Apart from the increase in rubbish-bin foxes and the cheering sight of a cock pheasant strolling down a Norwich main street in the small hours, it has been good to see red deer regularly in North Norfolk. Every winter I glimpse a few from the road.....eight hinds in the neighbouring sugar beet field two years ago, two stags blocking the road in the bitterly cold weather of last winter, occasional tracks in the snow and mud. Recently a superb 12-pointer has been haunting the same field. He emerges from the woods just before dusk and chews sugar beet within twenty yards of the road.

When I stop the car to look at him he stands proud and tall, as big and as fit as any Highland Royal, staring at us for a full minute before trotting off back to the woods. What does he do? Where does he go? What sort of a life does he lead? In Scotland the hills would have resounded with his roaring for weeks past as he made his challenge or protected his hinds from his rivals, and he would have shepherded his herd across the moors in broad daylight. In Felbrigg and Bodham woods there had been no report of roaring and for all my walking through and between the forest rides I've surprised red deer seldom in broad daylight. Presumably, like the roe deer, they lie camouflaged in the remotest undergrowth all day and come out to feed only at night. I saw a single hind in the same field a week or two ago, but no sign of a herd.

Was the huge stag a defeated herdmaster wandering disconsolately far from the scene of his disgrace? It seemed unlikely, to judge from his size and his prime condition. Had he grown soft on a diet of overmuch sugar beet, and was there a hint of middle-aged spread about that unusual weight and gloss? Had he adopted old-fashioned Norfolk ways and devoted himself to a monogamous existence after a stormy youth? Perhaps Ted Ellis could cast some light on the extent to which red deer in the farms and woods of North Norfolk have forsaken the habits of their cousins in Scotland - or perhaps he will tell us that it is the Scottish red deer which have deviated from older English customs.

Fine weather often persists hereabouts until October or November, and this seems to encourage the animal population. One Sunday a particularly fine coypu was splashing his way up the head water of the Glaven near Baconsthorpe Castle, where the stream is little more than a ditch; the stout beast was barely pretending to swim. The barn owl is back after a couple of years' absence, and he and the cat seem to be sharing in a bumper harvest of small rodents. In the red deer woods a grey - yes, not a red - squirrel was enjoying a last scamper.

This was the first I've seen in this part of Norfolk, and it worried me. Red squirrels have been plentiful here for years, but it seems to me that there have been far fewer around this year. Whether they have suffered from the cruel winter, or whether the grey squirrels are beginning to drive them out, as they have done in so many southern counties, it may be too early to say. Personally I hope they go back to the parks and gardens of the south west and don't compete with our native reds.

In September I thought I saw a red squirrel scrambling up the old apple tree in my garden. This was odd, because I am over a quarter of a mile from the nearest woods. A further look revealed that it was a stoat climbing with great confidence and agility. British mammals are much more versatile than one would imagine: stoats can swim well also, as can red deer and most mammals.

Some fifteen years ago, when younger and even more foolish, I was moved to translate my love for animals into heroic action. I was camping in September at the head of a Highland sea loch. An unusually high tide had cut off a sheep which had been grazing on the lush short grass which borders the sea near the mouth of a big burn. The terrified animal was bleating its heart out as the waters rose around its ever-decreasing island of grass. When the last blade of grass disappeared beneath the tide and the wretched animal looked as though it were walking Christlike upon the waters, I could stand it no more. I tore off my clothes, dashed out across the mud and the shallows, and swam across two hundred yards of bitterly cold and swirling tidal water. When I had almost reached the island, tired, chilled and breathless, I was in some perplexity as to how to rescue an oversized and panic-stricken sheep. Life-saving technique, holding its head above the water by the horns? Fireman's lift once I was in my depth? There was no glint of co-operation in the animal's eye. It was understandably uncertain about my intentions.

Just as I was landing and on the point of making a grab for it, the confounded beast solved the problem by hopping calmly into the sea. With its long and shaggy fleece spreading out and billowing round it like a giant mop, it swam swiftly and effortlessly to shore, beating my time for the return journey by a clear two minutes, as the mocking laughter of my family rang in my ears. It was my first and, I hope, my last attempt to earn a life-saving medal.

The Mad File

Do all the inhabitants of Norfolk receive strange letters? So regularly do I receive them that I keep a 'Mad File'.

Not long ago I was talking of this with a Norfolk rector. After capping each other's tales of unexpected correspondence, I thought that I might have finally outdone the rector: 'I bet you don't get obscene drawings from Peru!' I concluded triumphantly. But he did! We both received ill-drawn, unsigned, barely recognisable drawings of sexual organs on air mail letters posted from Peru. Some person with access to a list of rural bourgeois who might easily be shocked?

There is no end to the variety of my mail. I once received an application for a French teaching post from a Spaniard whose name was ten words long. He claimed to speak fluently eight languages. After listing ten mayors of townships of over 20,000 inhabitants who would act as referees, he elaborated on the contributions he would make to school sport in Britain - 'especially vasca, bolos, ping pongs and jumpings'. His only British referee provided a striking example of references between lines....interpret it as you will: 'This gentleman is Mephistophelian in appearance and has the manner of a Castillean grandee. You may be sure that he would make a memorable and lasting impression on any sensitive English youth whom he might be called upon to teach.'

On the whole I preferred the application of a Hongkong boy of (to me)uncertain age. 'Honoured and esteemed Sir, I beg the honour to submit my application to be considered for entry to your highly regarded College. My name is ----------, I was born in the fourth lunar month of the Year of the Horse. I wish to take A levels in Physics, Chemistry and Biology. May peace and prosperity attend your paths.' (He passed them at the highest grade!)

Not all letters are so calm in tone. One started 'In the year of Bel the Dragon 2000, Hell's Dungeon' and maintained its impetus to the end. One, purporting to come from a titled lady, was fifty typed pages long. After warning me about a papist plot against the Public Schools, for which, for some reason, responsibility was attributed to J.B.Priestley, Adenauer, de Gaulle, the Kennedys and Lord Pakenham, the lady broke into a rather oddly worded and versified song entitled 'Britannia and the dance of the seven veils'. There have been anonymous letters, even threats against my life, balanced by letters I will treasure always.

A Norfolk psychiatrist once told me that three per cent of the population would undergo hospital treatment for mental disorders at some stage of their life, and adolescents were especially vulnerable. He guessed that three or four times that number went through periods when they might benefit from expert help. Nearly 600 pupils and some 1500 parents with well over twice that number of ex-pupils will by the law of averages, in the course of 27 years of headmastering, produce a substantial number of lunatics, and an even larger number of eccentrics. With this clientèle a correspondence of 20 to 50 letters a day will inevitably throw up some unusual thinking. Nearly all these letters are recognisable by their florid handwriting - large, well-rounded letters with over-ornamented capitals, and all manner of scrolls and twirls. Words are underlined two or three times, and exclamations scattered in threes and fours.

Sometimes, instead of writing, the eccentrics present themselves in person. On the first day of a recent holiday, at 9 p.m., a man in his thirties rang my front door bell. He was dressed in shorts - Bavarian style lederhosen. Flowing blond hair was swept back from his temples like a youthful Einstein, and he had bright blue eyes. In his right hand he bore a five foot staff, from the top of which fluttered a banner with an image of the Virgin Mary. The overall impression he gave was of a cross between a boy scout and the prophet Elijah. He requested accommodation for the night, to which I agreed. When I enquired where he came from, he replied 'From God!' I will draw a veil over the complex events of the next 24 hours, except to say that he left shortly after offering to administer the 'kiss of holiness' to my wife.

The first day of the holidays must be a dangerous time. On a similar occasion, and at the same time of day, a gentleman with strange piercing eyes, an MI5 raincoat and a ten gallon hat asked me if he might have a quarter of an hour of my time. 'There is just one condition, Headmaster: may the interview take place back to back?' I was curious enough to grant his request, and placed chairs accordingly in my study. After showing me how he had come all the way from California seeing the world upside down and backwards via a careful arrangement of mirrors fitted to the underside of the brim of his hat, he tried to persuade me to make my pupils start every day by solving anagrams.

He then paused: 'Fetch me an apple, Headmaster,' he continued. I placed an apple on the floor as directed, whereat he waved his arm like a conjuror. An extensible fork at the end of a Heath Robinsonian arrangement of jointed metal and rubber bands shot out of his sleeve. Triumphantly he managed to spear the apple and steer it to his mouth. 'If you make all your pupils eat like this, Headmaster,' he observed, ' you will enable them to break through the crust of habit. That is the whole purpose of education.'

There was a streak of genius in his theory, but I did not buy his machine. I believe that I may miss some of these unexpected letters and visits when I retire. I hope my successor will be prepared..... Norfolk is not like other places!

Thanks to the Modern Clergy

It was sad to read in November an indirect attack on modern clergymen, contrasting them with the supposedly formidable parsons of past ages. The dear old Church of England's representatives and leaders have always been tempting targets from *Barchester Towers* to *Gas and Gaiters*, but they have never been more vulnerable than now. I have had a periodic crack at them myself, as they tackle the most difficult job in the world with dauntless courage and little appreciation.

No doubt there were fine men among the country parsons of old. These self-confident bastions of virtue usually came from a good family background. They lived securely (once the danger of being burned at the stake had receded) in lovely houses with domestic help. Their duties left them ample time to follow their interests. Apart from the hunting parsons and the porty prelates, most pioneer bird-watchers from the great Gilbert White to the present century were country vicars.

Even in the first half of the century, it was not a particularly stressful existence. A good parson was at the centre of village life, captaining the cricket team, keeping an eye on every social function, and presiding at Sunday services which were still community ocasions of importance.

There was little likelihood of loud and public denunciation of a parson's views; the Press, the B.B.C. and public opinion supported Christianty and its agents. For a modern cleric to command respect takes heroic efforts of a quite different order. He lives in a country which loves to grumble about its leadership, but has made itself almost unleadable.

In the first half of this century problems for parsons were growing, but the moral capital built up by Christianity still remained in the shape of general decency, even if it was crumbling and undermined. Soon after the last war, however, everything fell apart. Some of the decency was exposed as hypocrisy, and many hitherto accepted values tottered under almost universal challenge and questioning. The young changed within a few years, perhaps even a few months, from well-turned-out and obedient accepters to sullen, long-haired, graceless rebels. Nothing has been quite the same since. Many of the best and most intelligent of all ages began to shed their certainties....the world is no longer a certain place.

For those who had taken their ordination vows in the years before, the sixties and seventies must have been a time of terrible testing. Many must have been torn apart by internal struggles to retain their faith in the face of a society which seemed to reject all they stood for and of problems which had not existed when they were young. Some saw their churches emptying and their parishioners turn to violence and theft. The Pill, the bomb, irresponsible media and parents, and the massive scale of crime, changed the world.

Undermined by doubts, overwhelmed by the sufferings of the ever-incresing wrecks of the 'permissive society', they were seldom appreciated by people quicker to criticise than to help. Merely to survive needed heroism. To rise above it all, as some have done, to retain faith, courage, kindliness and good cheer is nothing short of miraculous. They have re-interpreted Christianity in the most adverse times, making it less pompous and hypocritical, no longer attempting to hurl people down the paths of righteousness, but stressing the need for loving kindness and understanding and service.

I have an instinctive aversion to homosexuality and do not want to see it encouraged, but the new Christians have shown us just how barbarous was our treatment of homosexuals in the self-righteous days of our forefathers.

If some of our modern Christian leaders have regrettably and ineffectually bleated like superannuated sheep, and even if some of the young ones may have appeared weak and wimpish, many have been a shining example of the power of Christianity in the darkest times. Less come forward for ordination, so the choice is not so wide. In their honest, tolerant, puzzled, but brave and kindly way, they have constantly defended the things which can make the world worth living in for our grandchildren.

Deeply conscious of similar stresses in the lives of headmasters over the same decades of accelerating change, and of my own failure to maintain the no longer tenable certainty and unassailable virtue of my forefathers, I would like at least to say a heartfelt thank you for the magnificent efforts of the best of our modern clergy. An alliance is desperately needed between the confused millions who have lost their sure faith, but not their dreams of a kindlier and more giving world, and the tentative, but honest, spiritual and compassionate interpreters of modern Christianity.

It would be pleasant to return to the formidable father figures of yore, but we have created a society in which their existence would barely be possible. If loving kindness has replaced intolerance, it may not be a move away from true Christian standards.

Beastly Statistics

In 1984, the last year for which statistics were available, the French shot 13 million thrushes: supposedly fieldfares, but including other varieties. When I read this alarming extract from a French conservationist bulletin to a chasseur friend, I raised a British bird-lover's eyebrow. He shrugged his shoulders. 'It represents barely one tin of thrush pâté per family per annum,' he said sadly. 'I expect the Italians get just as many.' I expect they do, if there are any left. The public sale of thrush pâté was made illegal in France last year, but the thrush remains the chasseurs' favourite victim.

It all depends on how you look at things, however. Statistics, especially about birds and beasts, are my favourite form of fiction. If you laid out all the world's statisticians end to end, it might not affect the world as profoundly as statistic fans might imagine, but it would deprive us of a lot of fun. At their best, natural history statisticians choose important subjects, quote sources, and are respectable. I enjoy their more erratic and intriguing speculations. 'If....

'If you released two wasps, one in Caithness and the other in Hampshire, and they both flew at random, the odds against their colliding would be less than the odds against any two particular stars hitting each other.' What a splendid picture, and how full of nonsense. I suspect it was a half remembered misquote from James Jeans. Sensible wasps no doubt seek to avoid collisions...has the statistician worked out the impact of sexual attraction or of the relative expectation of life of wasps and stars?

'If all the rats in the sewers under London and Paris were given tickets for the cup final and entitled to one human seat each, they could fill Wembley for two hundred and twenty successive days!' This has vintage charm, bringing home to our imagination a Lewis-Carrol-like picture of eager rats, rustling their programmes, tucking their tails under their arms, decked in Tottenham or Arsenal colours, craning their necks and squeaking in excitement, even if less likely than their human counterparts to invade the pitch. It is better than just telling us that London and Paris are believed to have between 15 and 30 million sewer rats!

'Every glass of tap water in London has passed through seven other human beings!' No wonder there is migration to rustic Britain, and no wonder someone is making money by selling Highland spring water.

The *Guiness Book of Records* has lost its power to surprise where mankind is concerned. The fact that a winner of the Dundee pork pie eating championship just after the war managed 56 station buffet pork pies in 50 minutes is astonishing only to those old enough to remember those monuments to ancient British digestion. Human beings are a very small part of the Scheme of Things - all humanity could be fitted on to the Isle of Wight if.........

The world of natural history offers more scope. 'If all the spores of a giant puff ball found the right temperature, soil and humidity, they could produce a mass of puff balls within a single season which would be bigger than the earth.' It makes one grateful for our erratic climate, which prevents mountains of white globes from engulfing East Anglian farms, or from burying the world before flying off into space like a shower of asteroids.

The desman (a rare and endearing little mammal only first discovered in Pyrenean streams in the nineteenth century) has the world's most sensitive snout. One million cells in its tender nose sprout a hair each. These bring detailed impressions of neighbouring objects, whether in dark, daylight or water, If you shaved the desman's nose it would be blind and helpless....

The statisticians tell us that the average British blue tit has nine chicks in a season. The odds are that just one parent and one chick will survive the winter. A power benevolent to sparrowhawks has decreed that the three weeks during which most baby blue tits are defenceless, leaving their nests only half capable of flight, is the time of year when sparrowhawk chicks are at their hungriest. So don't be impatient when the few surviving tits tap at the window in winter to remind you to refill the bird table. Strangely enough in countries where there are few predators, blue tits lay less eggs.....

The British are becoming increasingly enlightened and kind to their wild life. It is good to lie in an electric-blanketed British bed in April listening to our fat tame thrushes and blackbirds leading our unrivalled dawn chorus, and thanking God that Brits do not shoot 13 million of them. We should not, however, be too angry with the French, or with the child who occasionally steals one of those irresistible turquoise eggs freckled with black.. Let the statisticians console us. James Fisher once calculated that if every song thrush in Britain laid its maximum number of eggs every season, and if all survived to the maximum expectation of life of a song thrush and, in their turn, reproduced efficiently, within 13 years there would be so many song thrushes that for every one that could get a land purchase on the world, 150,000 would be hovering in hope of a place. That puts thrush pâté in a different perspective.

There is something called the 'balance of nature'. From time to time we adjust it with a nervous push one way or other, but we'd better be careful.

Don't be Frightened, Stand Still

Do you remember reading in some of those marvellous animal stories - *Lobo the Wolf* or *Jock of the Bushveld* or *the Jungle Book* - that no man need fear any beast as long as he remains calm and motionless and looks it in the eye? I have always tried to follow this advice, with varied results. Never having visited any of the exotic countries where I might have put my courage to the test by out-staring man-eaters, I started by practising at the Zoo. It was a disappointing venture. The gorilla wasn't interested in returning my steady infantile gaze, and it was quite impossible to catch the lion's eye at feeding time.

As the Big Game weren't playing, I turned my attention to lesser fry. The fact that I am lucky enough not to be afraid of some of our dumb chums which send my wife and daughters up the wall with horror and disgust, gives me a chance to show off. When a tarantula or a scorpion wanders across James Bond's hairy chest, and the cinema is filled with squeals of mingled terror and delight, I just raise a bored eyebrow, reminding my children in exasperatingly schoolmasterish style that Freud believes that there is no inborn or natural fear of snakes or spiders, we merely use them as a convenient focus for our own dark complexes. When spiders have to be lifted from the bath or scorpions or praying mantisses from the tent, I oblige.

But each man has his Waterloo. Mine, unfortunately and humiliatingly, is the common wasp. Its buzzing sends shivers down my spine; I have come to hate black and yellow, and I am even more frightened of its nasty tickling than of its vicious sting. To make matters worse, my wife is afflicted with such a perverse love of the beasts that in the family they are known as 'Mummy's stripey chums'. I watch with uncomprehending horror as she hospitably lets them crawl over her lips or extends a finger to rescue them from drowning in syrup or jam. In spite of her cries of 'Don't be frightened, stand still!', I jump to my feet as soon as one gets near me; either I run away, or I assault it with the mingled ferocity and cowardice which is born of panic, either with the flat of a carving knife (very sporting when they are on the wing) or with a rolled magazine. Even she will admit that she gets stung far more often than I, but any malicious satisfaction this might afford me is defeated by the infuriating way she smiles and says, with every appearance of sincerity, 'It really doesn't hurt at all, you know!'

However, I have otherwise continued to pursue my policy of superior and unflappable calm. There have been surprises. In Provence, when one of those big fat bush crickets landed on my ankle and I was lecturing my children on its harmlessness and beauty, it responded to my affectionate reception by giving me three or four astonishingly sharp nips. I was similarly put out when, going

65

to beg some water off a neighbouring farmer, I decided to show my children that there is nothing to fear from dogs if you move quickly and confidently, in spite of the notices that sprout everywhere about *chien méchant*. This particular *chien méchant* was about a foot long and it answered to my quick confidence and French baby-talk by attacking me unprovoked and with persistent savagery, ending by taking a chunk out of my trousers and my calf.

In the Highlands I was more successful, quelling aggressively curious bullocks with folded arms and fearful frown. Similar technique was, however, much less successful with a bull in the Lake District. Something about the look in its eye and the manner of its advance told me that discretion might be the better part of valour; my arms unfolded, my frown lost authority, and a calm backwards walk abruptly changed to a desperate forward gallop. I clambered over the loose stone wall with only a few feet to spare, and as I disappeared down the road he was still pawing at the top of the wall and scattering an avalanche of large stones on to the tarmac. N.B. except wasps, dogs and bulls.

One day in the Highlands two stoats were so lost in a deadly fight that they actually rolled together over my motionless foot as I stood and watched them. Years later I was to remember this incident. One of my children shouted, 'Look, Daddy, there's a rat! Don't let it get too near, it might jump up and bite you!'

'Nonsense!' I replied, 'Just old wives' tales. Keep still and they never harm you.' We all froze in our tracks, except for the rat which trotted straight up to my feet, climbed on to my shoe and shot straight up my trouser leg. There was an ugly struggle between instincts of self-preservation and faith. The children roared with laughter as, after some defensive groping, I undid the top of my trousers. Rather less scared than I after its precarious journey, the rat hopped out from the region of my navel.

Wasps, *chiens méchants* bulls and now rats. If I were you I should accept the advice of the old naturalists, if not with a pinch of salt, at least with decent caution.

66

Half a Thousand Clergymen

When my tax inspector hinted that it was no part of a headmaster's job to dispense alcohol to school guests, I pointed out that I had entertained my five hundredth cleric to lunch after chapel on Sunday. If I had not pandered to their understandable thirst after righteousness, I might have found it impossible to lure them out of the safety of their churches to face the most critical audience in the world - conscript teenagers.

Over five hundred clergy! It is the greatest possible tribute to them that, after nearly a quarter of a century, I look forward to the next batch with equanimity, or even pleasure, even if there have been downs as well as ups. Although sheer numbers and time have dulled many of my memories, so that we look back on a shadowy blur of ascetic or porty faces, black or purple robes, administrative or spiritual personalities, a few stand out. Many have been marvellous people whose lives have been transformed and irradiated by the cause they serve, but only a handful have had the ability to transmit a special spiritual power. They ultimately are the most complete proof of the existence and nature of God - it is through such glowing bulbs that the electricity makes itself most clearly visible.

Boys and girls, so often apparently apathetic or suspicious, recognise real saints. Their irreverence sees through pose and cant with X-ray eyes: mere vested interest in virtue cuts no ice, but they respond instinctively to what is genuine.

Like little Pastor Schultes. Alf Schultes was a German junker who quarrelled with his rich and powerful family, was thrown into a concentration camp for his outspoken views, and escaped to Britain. He arrived on our doorstep unannounced and unapologetic and asked if he could speak with the boys. He never failed to make a memorable impression, especially on those who were muddled or in trouble. He saw right into their difficulties and induced people who had never faced the truth to strip away all pretence. His soft voice and his Germanic accent made his sermons hard to listen to, but in group discussion he was unrivalled: profound and radical and wise.

He had no source of income, but prayer; no job but talking to people and helping them. An extraordinary mixture of old-fashioned aristocratic square and penniless revolutionary, he was able to get across to all classes and would turn people's habits, attitudes and prejudices upside down. He never asked for financial help, but it always came when needed. He dressed neatly and was a connoisseur of wine, but would fast unnoticed for days. At seventy-five his step was as springy as a boy's, and when he was dying of cancer of the stomach, his complete faith and peace were an inspiration to all. He was loved in schools,

Bishop Wilson of Birmingham was a big man whose presence was so generous and kindly that no one could fail to be happy if he was in the room. He had been tortured and beaten in a Japanese prisoner-of-war camp because he had kept Christianity alive among the starving, the sick and the dying; yet he converted his torturers, and found such joy and power as a result of his experience that they remained with him visibly to the end, and spilled over for the benefit of all who met him.

Sir George Trevelyan: not an ordained priest, but a prophet with a mane of white hair and brilliant blue eyes, so full of fire and vision and truth that he can still hold a young audience spellbound - because they know that he knows something, has something, is something that they have never experienced so vividly before.

Bishop Aubrey Aitken: full of gimmicks which, if others used them, might be off-putting. He has turned his disability into a great strength. Illness reduced his voice years ago to a hoarse whisper, which, boosted by microphones, rivets the attention of his congregations. Behind the showmanship and the rugby-player's frame is a personality of immense warmth and strength, full of boyish enthusiasm, tempered by a man's experience and suffering, lovable and true.

It would be embarrassing to go on. The impressive thing about most of them is their sheer humanity and selflessness, their humility and helpfulness often in the face of poverty, misunderstanding or even hostility. They are a great advertisement for their faith in difficult times.

What distinguishes the best of them? The common factor is undoubtedly suffering. Through suffering they have acquired understanding and power and the ability to help. Secondly, they are absolutely genuine and without pretence, and therefore completely trustworthy. Finally they are not concerned with laying down rules, making judgments, instructing us in black and white or listing prohibitions; they affect us by what they are more than by what they say.

Pastor Schultes was going one day to attend a meeting of Buddhists in London. A local clergyman wished him well and expressed the hope that he would be successful in converting some of them. 'That was not my idea,' replied Alf, 'I hope to be able to learn from them.'

I suspect the Buddhists learnt something from him too. I certainly did, and I am very grateful to him - and to the four hundred and ninety-nine others. People, and especially young people, find it awkward to say thank you, so that the indifferent or the critical are far more obvious, but I know how many of them share my gratitude and would like to be associated with my thanks. Their influence may have been largely unsung and unappreciated, but in a quiet way it has been prodigious.

Education 1

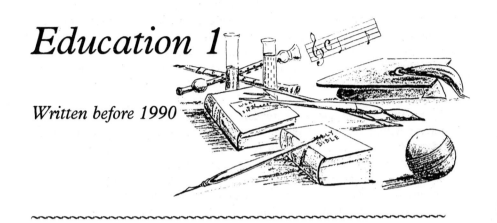

Written before 1990

No Room for Compromise

The finest education in the world could shortly be wrapped up in that sinister phrase 'integration with the state system' and buried in the name of egalitarian theory. The last rites will be so elaborately set about with commissions, reports and talk of reasonable compromise that the publc will not realise there is going to be a corpse to bewail, nor the victim understand that he is dying.

The basic principle on which the public schools stand is the most important bastion of democracy: freedom of choice in education. If the state does not provide enough boarding schools of quality and variety to meet the demand, someone else must. Each man should be free to buy what he likes if it does no harm to anyone else. If he earns good money, no one objects to his buying a Jaguar. The first step towards a 1984 nightmare of uniform levelling-down would be a state monopoly of education. And a state which forbids, on political or social grounds, a form of education highly commended by its own inspectors on educational grounds is well on the way to monopoly and tyranny: the anthill is at our door.

'It won't be so bad,' the moderates say, 'a British compromise will be reached; both parties will be satisfied with a wider entry.'

Freedom is not a matter for compromise.

A school is free only if it has the right to appoint and dismiss its own staff, to select and reject pupils, to frame its own time-table and rules, to spend the money available as it likes, to maintain the staff-pupil ratio it thinks appropriate and to conform to what religion it wishes. To abdicate any of these freedoms would be fatal. If the state controlled entry, it would probably insist on giving priority to the children of divorced parents. The schools would be glad to help, but too high a proportion would change their character fundamentally. Any schoolmaster will tell you that 90 per cent of his disciplinary and moral problems come from such children. We do not want to become homes for mixed-up kids; nor would it be fair, either on those children or on the others.

We have always wanted to broaden our entry: successive governments have refused help. Every schoolmaster would rather teach the intelligent or even the adaptable sons of the poor than the stupid sons of the rich. Unconditional grants to those who need, or want and deserve public school education would be welcome to all . But not at the expense of freedom. We might be asked to change our staffing ratio to conform with the state system. But one cannot run a good boarding school on a staffing ratio adequate for a day school.

The essence of good education is variety; a state monopoly cannot provide this. The public school 'system' covers a multitude of educational ideas from Bedales to Uppingham, from Dartington Hall to Atlantic College, from Sevenoaks to Gordonstoun. If you prefer Calvin and the cane to French and free expression, or co-education and contraception to scholarship and straw hats, what right has your government to say no?

We would be the first civilised western democracy to ban independent boarding schools. They flourish in America, New Zealand and Australia and no one in these genuinely democratic countries accuses them of being a 'divisive force in the life of the nation'. Only in England are efficiency and success such a focal point for jealousy and resentment.

The usual charges are:

First: It is unfair that the rich should buy a good education which is not available to the poor.

Second: Public school education constitutes a privilege that ensures entry to Oxbridge, the Services and the Foreign Office.

Third: They are out of date. Their buildings are archaic, they prefer Greek to science, and are not even academically superior to the grammar schools.

Fourth: According to the Left, they inculcate middle-class attitudes to religion, sex and politics. They reduce boys' ability to question and criticise. They have ridiculous rules about not smoking and drinking. They wear uniform, and they 'encourage an exaggerated respect for private property'.

Fifth: They are supposed to be hotbeds of sadism, homosexuality, class-consciousness, racialism, games-mindedness, repressive tyranny, hypocrisy and emotional sterility. They teach leadership through power, instead of persuasion; they humiliate the weak through fagging and corporal punishment, and they provide a hell of discomfort for the sensitive, the original and the creative. They promote ineptitude and stifle genius.

We are guilty of the first charge. Although some of us get little help from LEAs, or the Ministry, we give as many scholarships as we dare to attract the able poor. The solution might be to give educational grants to parents which could be used at any school of their choice. These would be increased above the basic according to need and merit.

Most of the other charges are the result of emotional attitudes. The public schools' supposed monopoly of Oxbridge entries no longer applies. Apart from the irritating injustice of closed scholarships, which in any case now usually demand standards as high as open awards, the two reasons for public school preponderance are merit and the shortage of maintained school candidates. To quote the Senior Tutor of Trinity College, Cambridge: 'We could not have chosen other than we did, unless we were prepared to take weaker candidates on political grounds.' The Services and Foreign Office interview boards bend over backwards to be fair and to make allowances for boys of differing backgrounds. As at Oxbridge, there is a shortage of state school applicants because they *believe* the legend that they will be at a disadvantage.

Some schools are out of date, others not. Science equipment is often first-class, and bias towards classics dying. Some of their experimental and pioneering work has been spectacular, and the top public schools get academic results second to none, although some of their intake is below eleven-plus standards.

What is a 'middle-class attitude towards sex'? The middle classes, like most others, are in favour of it; which does not exclude trying to project a high ideal for love and marriage. As for religion and politics, a schoolmaster's concern is not with sect or party. He just tries to get his pupils to ask themselves not 'Is it profitable? Is it modern? Is it popular?' but 'Is it true or false, beautiful or ugly, right or wrong?' Fortunately we are as powerless to deaden the modern boy's ability to question and criticise as anyone else. If anyone thinks he can indoctrinate them with middle-class attitudes by tyrannous methods, he misjudges the generation. The more reactionary and tyrannous the attitude, the more lively and questioning the criticism. The satire movement, for better or worse, started in the public schools.

Alas! We fail conspicuously to teach 'an exaggerated respect for private property', as anyone who knows the wholesale 'borrowing' that goes on in public schools would confirm. Discouraging the young from drinking and smoking is not a cause for shame, and although the day of school uniform may be nearly over, its praiseworthy intention is to minimise differences of background and wealth.

There remain the exaggerated charges of corporal punishment, fagging, snobbishness, bullying, homosexuality etc. An intelligent case can be made out for corporal punishment in adult hands and limited to a few clearly-defined offences. A good prefect punishes little, but needs great unselfishness and skill in human relationships. Modern fagging is a badly needed training in service and domesticity. It is good, as every mum knows, for sons to learn to tidy up and wait at table. Public schoolboys are no more snobbish, brutal and sadistic than teenagers the world over. They mix with boys of different regions, countries and class; perhaps more than grammar schoolboys who are often confined to the intelligentsia of a single provincial town. Some come from snobbish homes; we try to overcome this handicap. Remember, however, that to the man who blows his nose in his fingers, the man who uses a handkerchief is a snob. Boys can be horrible to one another, and our most difficult task is to ensure that a boy who is 'different' does not get levelled down. At least we are aware of the problem and control it more efficiently nowadays.

Homosexuality occurs amongst teenage males whatever the circumstances. It is less of a problem today. School monasticism is less strict than formerly, and there is often some co-operation with girls' schools. Love, however, is not always a help to work; there *are* four months of holidays.

The public schools have failures and weaknesses. But boarding schools with good masters provide a range of spare-time interests (artistic, technical and creative as well as sporting) impossible in any other community. They keep alive the fading ideal of educating the whole man - heart, imagination, body and mind - and develop a strong sense of responsibility to the community. By casting the net of opportunity wide, they hope to find something to stimulate enthusiasm, to offer challenge and to provide success for any boy. And this is of equal importance to developing his powers of questioning and criticism.

Whatever the results (and they are often brilliant), our aim is the highest. We are trying to build bridges between the warring factions of a muddled world; between a puzzled church and its lost congregations, between black and white, class and class, nation and nation, illiterate technologist and impractical arts man, haves and have-nots, stuck-in-the-mud trade unionist and out-of-date management.

Perhaps we fall short: 'who shoots at the midday sun, though he be sure he shall never hit the mark; yet as sure he is he shall shoot higher than he who aims but at a bush.' Our faithful clientèle who believe we offer those very ideals which our country most lacks at the moment, and who make formidable sacrifices to send their children to us, may be misguided but they deserve to be

72

left alone! If the independence of the public schools ends, it will be a deadly blow to education in the name of class resentment and will represent another decisive and perhaps fatal step down the slippery slope from a great liberal democracy to a petty back-biting and decadent little bureaucracy.

New Dirty Word

Elitism has become a dirty word which conjures up all kinds of irrelevant emotions. It is constantly misused to suggest discrimination in favour of a traditional ruling caste, with overtones of resentment. All it really means is the selection of the most talented people for appropriate jobs. In this sense Britain needs élites more than at any time in her history and it is a teacher's duty to create as wide a variety of élites as he can.

The pursuit of a misconception of equality is more responsible than anything for the plight of Britain. A compassionate society must be based on the creation of wealth by the talented and the hard-working to support the unfortunate and the untalented: if it becomes a society for the promotion of the loud and the aggressive, and the restriction of the clever and the industrious, then all is lost. A Russian factory worker who increases output receives a citation and is made a hero of the Soviet Union: an Englishman who does so is just as likely to be sent to Coventry. A small boy who has the misfortune to be interested in French or classical music is laughed at by his mates for being 'snobby' and, for his own protection, learns to pretend to an interest in pop music and football fanaticism instead.

In Russia the pick of the school children in towns and villages where maths teaching is inadequate are sent to boarding schools where the best maths teachers can get the best out of the pick of the bunch - because, as the education chief of a Soviet department said in 1975, 'We ignore the talent of youth at our peril; of such gold is the future of our country made.' In Cuba and East Germany talent is sought out and developed from the earliest age.

Only in Britain is brilliance at all levels of society regarded with suspicion and success with cynicism. Of course brilliance survives in a few corners, but wherever it is detected it risks being branded as élitism, or is cut down to size by the professional debunkers of the media.

This is not a question of class. Ask the dockers or the Coventry car workers whether they want the best for their children or whether they would like to see rewards for hard work and skill. We need an élite of highly-paid, highly efficient workers with substantial shares in their own firms; an élite of modern and progressive management; an élite of inventors, scientists and technologists; an élite of games players, craftsmen, artists, dancers, labourers, shopkeepers and politicians. I don't want to be represented at Westminster by someone who is my equal, but by someone whose knowledge and understanding of public affairs is far superior to mine. If I seek the help of an electrician, a plumber, a carpenter, a dentist, a surgeon, a secretary or a restaurateur, I don't want someone who is average, but a person of the highest ability and qualifications.

The life of schoolteachers should be dedicated to the creation not of an élite but of a mass of élites. Parents send us children so that they may, if possible, master the three Rs and become mannerly, disciplined, unselfish, courageous and kind - not to express their tiny egos and run the schools according to their liking. We seek to meet the parents' desires in this respect and not those of the children, although we should be stupid to be out of touch with their ideas.

Beyond this, most of us (I hope, though I am not, alas, certain) aim to discover each child's talents and to push them as far as their abilities will take them. In every group of boys we must convince ourselves that there may be a George Best, an Einstein, a Benjamin Britten, a skilled mechanic, a pop star, a tycoon, a brilliant chef, a gifted linguist, a strong man or a saint. The teacher must turn and twist and struggle to find the key which will unlock each child's dedication and enthusiasm and, having found some first signs of potential, hang on to them like a bulldog.

In every worthwhile subject or achievement, from joinery to hurdling, or from music to maths, there are successive barriers of difficulty which hold up all but the most stout-hearted. The teacher's task is to push each student through these barriers which, once surmounted, will open up new fields of happiness and success.

Over the door of each College of Education the words should be written: 'My first duty is to get the best out of each child.'

Of course this is idealism. The horrid truth confronting teachers in a bad slum comprehensive may make it seem like cloud cuckoo land. But these children also have potential, given a firm lead and the assumption that they can succeed. If they have no academic potential, they can be climbers, racing drivers, footballers, boxers, adventurers.

Academic élites are neither the most valuable nor the most important: dons are often absent-minded and incompetent outside their own specialities, and I am overcome with humility at the sight of an expert butcher, embroiderer, electrician, gardener or builder - as I hope some of them may be at the sound of my fluent and accurate French.

What is wrong about society is that it creates false élites on grounds of cash, nepotism or accent, while ignoring more genuine forms of élite. What causes

74

indignation is the spectacle of unpleasant jobs, high skills, devoted services and hard work unrewarded. The remedy for that is in the hands of the government and the industrial negotiators, not in social engineering in the schools. While schools must devote a large share of their energies to the apparently slow and lazy, they must not let the powerful trade union of the failed and resentful, or the imbecile guild of progressive theorists, deflect them from their first job - which is, and must remain, the creation of élites.

It is a hard and competitive world and will remain so; if we fail to prepare boys and girls for it we do them a disservice.

Egregious Applications

Someone, they tell me, has at some stage given professional advice to every qualified applicant for a teaching post about how to apply.

I can't believe it. After 27 years of sorting out applications to draw up short lists for interviews, no eccentricity can surprise me.

Not that perfection of presentation is a guarantee. One of the most skilled presenters of the post-war period was a self-styled reverend gentleman with a first at Keble. He was, in fact, neither ordained, nor the possessor of a degree; but he obtained (among others) posts as a Lecturer at Toronto University, as a History teacher at Scotch College, Adelaide and two other Public Schools, as Vice-Principal of the Theological College of Columbo, and as Lecturer in Modern History at Oxford. This exciting career was only briefly interrupted by an excursion into bigamy and a prison sentence.

Nevertheless, crisp presentation is a help, as anyone will testify who has waded through letters of application of the expansive autobiographical type: Page after page of self-centred and self betraying gush.

Much preferable was the brevity of the applicant for a history post in a boys boarding school which started: 'Dear Sir, I am 6 foot 2, with blue eyes and curly hair and very fond of boys...' One knew where one was....

If a headmaster has a staff of 40 or so, he may well be dealing with two lots of applications simultaneously. They may coincide with the end of term when he has 500 or 600 reports to write, a sermon to preach and an infinite number of crises to deal with. His trials are not lessened even when the short list has been established. If he is unlucky enough to live in a remote corner of Britain, not only must he meet the expenses of his candidates, but he will have to suffer them for two or three meals and the night.

Every such headmaster must be familiar with that sinking feeling as another unwashed and jaded candidate emerges winkle-pickered from the taxi. 'Not another...' he will mutter to himself, pray silently for patience and steel himself to face 16 hours of polite farce with a candidate who is clearly no good and whose referees have obviously told white lies.

I do not forget my own first experience of being interviewed for an assistant master's job after the war, when I descended on the headmaster of a leading public school complete with wife and daughter. After being late for breakfast, my three-year-old daughter incurred the displeasure of the headmaster's wife by crawling into the dog basket. On being told to get out, she looked up rebelliously and said, loud and clear: 'Oh, B.......!' It seemed futile to explain that these were almost her first words and that we had no idea where she got them from! It does much credit to the broadmindedness of at least one headmaster that I got the job!

It may be easier for all concerned to have candidates put up in the local pub. But this, too, has its dangers. This was once done for an intending art master, and the official interview was arranged for 9 a.m. At 9.30 the telephone rang and a weary voice was heard: 'Ay say! Is that the head man? Do you mind awfully if ay don't turn up for a whale? Ay'm feeling a trifle bent this morning!' He could draw like Rembrandt and was appointed, but his subsequent career involved a fondness for the bottle and a colleague's wife. I believe he gave up teaching for the more rewarding pursuit of high art.

There are professional interviewers and amateurs. After a brief flirtation with officer selection board techniques, elaborate score sheets and Committees, I go for the amateur approach. Under this system, the Head of the Department gives a technical grilling. Once one has discovered that intending teachers in French can graduate from one of our most famous universities with accents like Churchill's and no ability to converse in the language, one tends to impose one's own standards. My brilliant Head of Maths used to grill and reject candidates with top honours because they could not explain their way through difficult A level questions.

There are other questions hammering away in the headmagisterial mind, and perhaps they should be known to the victims: Is he a man? Is he a gentleman? (Not a matter of accent , school or way of holding a teacup!) Will he be able to keep excellent order effortlessly? (So much more important than his theories about education!) Will boys admire him? Will his interests be a boon to your school? Will he cut ice with men and women as well as with boys? Has he a sense of humour? Will he be able to avoid turning into a narrow, dehydrated 40-year-old husk of a teacher? Will he give 100 per cent without looking continually to see what he is going to get out of it? And even, though this would not necessarily be decisive (otherwise one's supply would soon dry up altogether), is he by any chance an intelligent Christian?

The unfortunate candidate is ushered in to see the Head again. After demanding an assurance that the candidate will do anything at any time without expecting financial reward, the Head investigates spare time interests and accomplishments of potential value. This involves, for instance, confirming that 'enthusiasm for football' means watching the T.V., 'moutaineering' means a trip up the Snowdon railway, and 'artistic interests' means a teenage trip to a gallery with a rich aunt. After that session come the Real Tests: half an hour with an attractive secretary to 'ask her questions about the administration of the school', a time with the Headmaster's spoilt and unattended children and dog, a tour of the school with a senior pupil. Finally a session during which alcohol is poured into his exhausted frame to see what unguarded veritas emerges in the vino.

If he survives he will at least be tough (a primary requirement). If he actually impresses Head of Department, pretty Secretary, spoilt child, observant wife of Head, senior boy (most important) and is not bitten by the dog, he will have observed his job. If he accepts, he will be set for a life time of comparative poverty and gross overwork, relieved by lasting rewards and happiness.

Scraps of Paper

Teachers have been busy this last year or so rumbling and grumbling about exams. This seems to reach a peak about every ten years, but the huffing may have some effect this time.

About time too. The huge structure of our examination system is so complex that it threatens to become unchangeable, or to change so slowly that it will always be out of date. But change must not end competitive exams. Genii of our generation may be able to teach genii of the next without the incentive of exams and the discipline of the well-constructed courses which flow from them and lead to them; but genii are very rare. Boys and girls need that incentive and competition, and most teachers with their feet on the ground understand this. And although they are too slow to change, our exams are generally fair, incorrupt, efficient and well-organised.

What is wrong is not so much the examinations as the disproportionate importance attached to them. Parents, pupils, teachers and even some employers have begun to believe that O levels taken at 16, A levels at 18 and the class of honours degree taken at 22 provide a precise classification of standard and employability: a label and a place in the hierarchy for life.

These examinations provide no such thing. They are scraps of paper indicating that in late adolescence and early adulthood a pupil was more or less competent at taking academic examinations in specific subjects and was more or less well taught. Those labels give little guidance to the all-round talents of a 35-year-old. The age of 16 is, expecially for males, the worst age for taking exams. It is the stage of maximum muddle and 'all change'

Some jobs require a basic humble guarantee of numeracy or literacy, or both. A few require the academic ability; but even in this scientific age, they are few. Most successful people, even scientists, engineers and doctors, will tell you that they have never needed three-quarters of the information acquired at school and university: its main value was as mental training and discipline.

Sir Christopher Cockerell, who invented the hovercraft, was not an outstanding academic, he was an inspired fiddler. Some men and women with first class honours degrees renounce interest in their subject once there are no more exams to pass. Inventivity, creativity, imagination, personal warmth and charm, practical ingenuity, manual dexterity, money sense, determination...the list of great qualities unmeasured by exams is endless.

Because of the extravagant importance attached to exam qualifications, they are being required in totally unnecessary and irrelevant spheres. There is a danger that every cook, mechanic, musician, actor, games teacher, dancer, salesman and farmer will be made to pass written examinations. We already have to face the anomaly that a first-rate linguist will not qualify as a teacher without O level maths. Yet most of us could point to great chefs without O level domestic sciences or English; great historians without a qualification in History, practical field naturalists of tremendous knowledge without O level biology. What Molière said in the 17th century of pedants remains true: 'I live on tasty soup and not on fancy words.' And Malherbe and Balzac, so strong on grammar rules, in kitchen arts and skills might well have been mere fools!

Because I liked exams, I once passed a car maintenance course with first-class grading. Yet only a fool would entrust his car to me in the event of a breakdown. I am ham-handed and technologically incompetent, and watch qualified mechanics with astonished admiration as they diagnose infallibly and strip and repair intricate gadgets with deft skill.

The narrowness of merely academic teaching is one of the reasons why the film *Kes* has had such a wide impact. The hero is a boy rejected as incompetent by most of his teachers, companions and relations: a dreamer, ineffectual in class and on the games field. Yet his passionate devotion to the training of a kestrel brings out his latent patience, determination, skill, sensitivity and love. Children, like adults, sense how limited, artifical and clumsy academic qualifications have become as a measure (which they were never intended to be) of the infinite variety of life skills.

So, although I wish well to the exam changers and to the inevitable laureates of the examination halls, I wish even better fortune to campaigners for school profiles which will give more detailed and sensitive assessments of pupils' potential in all kinds of non-academic spheres. At the least they should lead to a greater awareness on the part of teachers, and to a closer interest in all the unexpected latent talents of pupils.

Most of all I hope that sensible bosses will appoint the best man or woman for the job in the full realisation that scraps of paper giving examination results are just valuable pieces of evidence: in no way the most conclusive, or the final basis for selction.

Testing Time for Teachers

Did you, in your youth, experience a gleeful thrill of anticipation when you heard you were going to have a new teacher? When served up with a genuine beginner, all apprehension and knocking knees, the 'lads' would either wait for him or her to trip up before they pounced, or lay elaborate traps.

The law of the blackboard jungle has always decreed that bad teachers must go through hell. Pupils have an unerring and merciliess ability to identify the weak, or the pompous or the inept. Some new masters were chivvied into leaving the profession, some struggled on through a lifetime of unhappiness, some sought advice and rose above it, some changed school and found no difficulty in a new setting. Many never had a moment's difficulty.

The most successful tended to be those who kept their pupils on their toes and busy from the start, never losing the initiative. The Revd Waddy at Rugby School, long years ago, is said to have started his first lesson with the words: 'I understand that it is the custom at this school to allow every boy the chance of one warning before he may be beaten: you are all warned!'

Another beginner in the same school was less effective. One of the senior boys had been irritating him with facetious questions. The young teacher finally turned on him. 'Right, James! If you're so clever, here's my gown, take over the class and see if you can do better!' James took the gown, took the teacher's place on the rostrum, leaned forward and addressed the expectant class: 'In recognition of my unexpected promotion to be in charge, and in view of your exceptional work this term, you may have the rest of the period free. Return to your houses at once.' Before the teacher could recover his wits, the entire class had escaped and dispersed at irretrievable speed.

I am conscious of how lucky many of us in the independent schools were. At least most children wanted to learn. I've watched colleagues who were friends and relations struggling with big town comprehensives. At times their problems were formidable. One male teacher, in his first term, found that his class had disappeared. A neighbouring master had commandeered his pupils, without even mentioning the fact to him or to the head, to accompany him on a protest march quite unconnected with education.

At another comprehensive, a large boy had become unmanageable because he organised a gang of bullies. Finally, when he had slugged several new prefects, the staff threatened to strike if the boy were not removed from the school. The governors refused to allow the head to take such action: the boy happened to be black, and they could not face the possible consequences.

Rather longer ago, a woman teacher in a big town school found her loyalties divided. A colleague organised a lecture to 11-year-olds on 'the black power martyr, Angela Davies'. After this the youngsters were sent round their parents their parents with collecting boxes. When the parents complained, the head rashly suggested that this teacher should have the courtesy to consult him on the invitation of outside lecturers, so that a balance could be maintained. Whereupon a staff meeting, without the head, was called to establish whether they should strike against this unwarrantable interference with their liberties.

Academic distinction is no guarantee against the 'treatment'. Distinguished scholars are often sufficiently unwordly to get the bird more decisively than their colleagues, whose feet are more firmly on the ground. One clever physicist soon after the war had a first and a blue, but he had only been at school a week or two before his normally well-behaved pupils were playing cards openly, with their backs to the blackboard, while he rambled incomprehensibly on. Another fine scientist retired early to avoid being shut in his own laboratory cupboards. It gave him time to write a valuable book on teaching.

In both cases the boys were right; these brilliant men were hopelessly disorganised and incoherent teachers. It has always been and always will be so. Fortunately there will also always be a supply of teachers who keep order effortlessly, and without having to resort to punishment or raised voices.

One thing is sure; neither examinations nor teachers' training colleges can offer any certain guide as to which they will be.

In Pursuit of the Unteachable

More dangerous even than the economic difficulties of Britain is the crisis in education. It is far too serious to be a political matter, or to be viewed from political angles.

The dimensions of the collapse of discipline and of effective education in the big cities and especially in London are concealed. To begin with, such things cannot be expressed in statistical terms and are therefore incapable of proof. If they could be so presented, the relevant statistics could not be available for some time and would then be much less significant even than political polls. Secondly, political and theoretical support for comprehensive schools is, understandably, so widespread that facts which don't fit or are inconvenient are wished away or shrugged off.

In the meantime the divisions in British society, already serious, are being widened, perhaps beyond repair, for the rising generation. A great many, in some areas a majority, of children are being brought up in an atmosphere hostile to work. They are suspicious of adults, resentful of success and possessed by destructiveness. Experience teaches them that effort is pointless, virtue unrewarded, and that the quickest way to gain admiration is to take a lead in knocking the establishment.

What has gone wrong? Were town schools in underprivileged areas always like this? The notion that the worsening of the situation is the invention of journalists who have merely taken the lid off a saucepan whose contents always smelt nasty is not tenable.

The first mistake has been the increase in the size of schools. The creation of schools of over 1,000 pupils in difficult areas in a permissive age was an act of bureaucratic folly. Any experienced teacher knows that very big schools only succeed with a good staffing ratio and good teaching in favoured districts. Where members of the staff do not know each other, much less parents or pupils, a blackboard jungle is inevitable.

The second problem is the salary of the teachers. There is no excuse for not paying substantial special allowances to attract strong and experienced teachers to the crisis areas. The high rate of turnover and the shortage of staff is snowballing to a point where delay may make it irreversible. The pupils have no motivation. Those of their parents, who have no educational quali-fications, are usually earning more than their teachers.

Believing in the pursuit of material advantages and personal comfort as the sole sensible aim, the pupils are asked to undertake unfamiliar and unsympathetic tasks which will apparently only fit them to become as underprivileged as their teachers. In many of these schools only a trickle take O levels, even less As. Those students who in their last year are not truants are in large part malcontents who can only be entertained by those teachers who find them good material for the fermentation of anarchical revolution or who amuse them at their own level.

This is just one aspect of the third problem: the raising of the school-leaving age. Never was there a clearer case of a good thing readily accepted by all good-hearted planners and writers turning out to be obviously harmful in practice: harmful to all but a minority of boys and girls, who would in any case have stayed on, harmful to the morale of teachers called on to teach the unteachable, and disastrously harmful to finances which might otherwise have provided more and better teachers.

The fourth problem is the nature of the teacher-training colleges. In a period of 20 years of interviewing school-teching candidates I have seldom discovered anyone who had praise for the training he had received. The fortunate exceptions stand out like jewels in a pile of coke. Problems of classroom control are often airily dismissed as irrelevant, details of syllabus and method glossed over by sadly inexperienced lecturers. The shadow of Jean Jacques Rousseau (who had the wisdom to warn us specifically against the disastrous consequences which would follow any attempt to apply in schools his ideas which were developed for an ideal tutor of an ideal boy) still darkens the common sense of those who devise their programmes.

The belief is still fostered that children born good and free must not be corrupted by civilisation, warped by constraint, or cramped by disciplined work. Given lots of expensive educational toys and an adequate supply of plasticine, they will blossom into self-expression and integrated personalities.

While there are some benefits which have come from these doctrines in liberalising some fairly dusty primary schools, (such as the acceptance of that useful generalisation, 'We hear and we forget, we see and we remember, we do and we understand,') the general impact has been disastrous. A generation has moved into the big comprehensives which could have survived only if they had been brilliantly taught and fitted into a highly organised and motivated environment.

In the event, the majority of the intake in the slum areas is incapable of exercising concentration. They have never been made to do anything which is not immediately congenial. The idea of short-range effort and sacrifice for long-range benefit is utterly foreign to them. They, in a word, do not know how to work or learn, for the simple reason that nobody has ever made them do so; a tragedy not of their own making, and only partially due to the decline in ambitious home influence.

Grave, and perhaps impertinent, charges for a man to make who is teaching in a privileged situation in a rural area. I can only say by way of defence that they are based on the experience of close relatives teaching in schools faced with some of these difficulties. It is also based on the experience of many colleagues, of whom I offer no criticism and for whom I feel the sharpest sympathy. It would be perfectly possible to fill this short article with horror stories. Unfortunately the fact that they are true would not make them either believable or significant. The consolation that individual schools are still doing a heroic and successful job must not blind us to the reality of the disaster. There have been improvements here and there in teaching the able and the handicapped children, but the average child succumbs.

To abolish good and successful schools in the hope that the bright boys and girls and able teachers will flood into the big city comprehensives and cure the situation would be to try to improve vinegar by pouring a little wine on to the top. The myth that the average boy is inspired by a hard-working minority has at last given way to the chill realisation of the truth which has always been evident to schoolmasters: a bad majority will corrupt all but the very exceptional members of the motivated minority. Where schools have not succumbed, they should be supported and protected.

It is no good moaning and criticising. What can be done? First, release the reluctant last year rebel - conscripts. At a stroke money is raised and the staffing situation improved, and atmosphere lightened. Second: the pay for teachers in crisis areas should be increased at once. Third: no lecturer should be appointed in any teacher-training college without highly successful experience of teaching for at least five years; the syllabus of the colleges should be revised. Perhaps implementation of parts of the James report will help. Lastly: leviathan schools should be broken up, unless they are particularly skilfully purpose-designed and actually proving successful; they should be decentralised and humanised and the staffing ratio improved from money saved from superfluous hardware and the many fatty areas of higher education.

If action is not taken now and given the highest financial priority, the second half of the seventies will see an increasing degree of uncontrollable ignorance and violence.

Today's school failures, anti-authority, anti-establishment, anti-social, are the disrupters of tomorrow. To carry out reforms would be barely half the battle. To put the big town social environment straight will need an even bigger fight. But that is another story.

Choosing Doctors

As medical science enters upon another decade of swift advance, are doctors improving in proportion? While some of us have splendid and dedicated doctors, many people feel that something has gone badly wrong at the base of the pyramid. That something could be the human touch, the reassurance of a wise philosopher and friend, or even that much-derided old-fashioned accomplishment, the bedside manner.

Achievement at the top is marvellous. Lives are saved which would have been lost 20, or even 5 years ago by the development of unbelievably skilled techniques. There are new machines and new drugs. Old diseases have been conquered and the spread of new ones checked; but the brilliant technical achievements at the top go hand in hand with a rather frightening bureaucratic infrastructure, which can be inhuman or even inefficient.

One must not entirely blame the general practitioner. In order to get where he is, he has had (if he is a young man) to get the highest A level grades, and to survive a long specialised training. This early concentration on scientific subjects does not help him to acquire knowledge of the world or of the arts or literacy or persuasiveness. Modern patients are more difficult than they were; a little knowledge has ensured that they are more often neurotic and critical than grateful and co-operative. A high proportion of the G.P.'s time is spent listening to the complaints of unhappy ladies in middle life, to frightened young men who read too many medical textbooks for their peace of mind, and to lonely folk whose symptoms are mainly a cry for help. It is not surprising that the constant cries of wolf may lead him to drop his standards or to be careless or impatient; he has too little time to hold hands, to advise, and to encourage. The quality he needs today is not primarily the capacity for top academic or scientific qualifications, but the ability to bear other people's negative emotions, without losing his kindliness, balance, sensitivity, and judgment in the face of suffering.

If this is so, why are G.P.s now recruited almost exclusively from those who gain top A level grades in science? Many experienced doctors will tell you that this policy is failing, because of the number of candidates of inappropriate character whose high grades at school do not apparently help them to distinguish themselves in the later stages of the medical course. One dean of admissions said to me: 'Presumably we get the best and brightest of schools' output, but certainly it is remarkable how dull and apathetic they can be when they are actually on the course.'

I doubt whether medical schools get the best or even the brightest of our output. In recent years my school has sent about 15% of its university candidates with 3 Bs or better towards medicine - certainly less than to engineering. The grades demanded ensure that they are academically- at that stage - among the brightest, but not necessarily the best. Most teachers will admit that a number of their top-grade scholars are complex, neurotic, unmotivated people, afraid of responsibility, lacking integrity, without the human touch, unwilling to work overtime, liable to crack under stress, and unlikely either to care for their patients or to inspire them with confidence. A few medical schools - particularly the London hospitals - have dared to rely on interviews, and to offer places to highly motivated students of character, subject to 3 Cs. Others are apparently guided only by A level grades.

Of course, some top brains are needed, and A grades with distinction give some guidance in seeking them. But every teacher and most university selectors should know that the difference between D and B grades may be a question of luck. It may depend on whether the candidate was lucky enough to revise the right questions, on the quality of his teaching at the vital moment, on the fortunes of a first love affair, on the phases of the moon (especially in the case of female candidates), or on the state of the candidate's digestion. It is indispensable evidence , but it must be taken in conjunction with many other facts: the age of the candidate and the stage at which he or she was promoted (a facet sadly neglected by most deans of admission); the degree to which his grades may have been due to memorising (a faculty to which A levels attach an importance fast becoming quite disproportionate); the success which the candidate has gained in other worthwhile activities, and the time and energy he has devoted to them (has he got a Duke of Edinburgh gold? Does he play the 'cello?), whether father and grandfather were doctors; the degree to which he may be better at projects or research than at exams. Finally, are there any indications as to whether the candidate has the makings of wisdom, resilience, judgment, emotional balance, courage, integrity and determination?

Doctors are not generally officers or civil servants. But medical schools could benefit from taking some elements from the Services' selection methods, even if the qualities they are seeking are not identical. The number of applicants prohibits complex and lengthy interviews for all candidates. Nevertheless better doctors would certainly be selected if teachers were made to report in detail on character as well as academic ability.

Perhaps this could be on a seven-point scale: outstanding, good, rather above average, average, rather below average, poor, hopeless - as applied to moral courage, motivation, determination, sense of humour, persuasiveness, integrity, steadiness under stress, physical energy, manual dexterity, width of interests, tact, ability to work in a team, ability to work by oneself. Guidance would have to be given; they would have to be judged by comparison with other 6th-formers in the school of origin, and the size of the school's 6th form would have to be indicated. This report should then be cross-checked by subjecting the candidates to groups discussions, lecturettes, or games devised by psychologists. A group of seven could be presented with the facts of a case and be left to pool their knowledge and work towards a solution in the presence of the interviewers. Perhaps one problem should involve medicine, one should involve organised thinking of a general kind, and one should involve familiar contemporary problems. Another alternative would be to present candidates with a medical problem, together with a number of papers providing the necessary information, and to ask them to explain their recommendations and to defend them.

The snags are obvious. The Services devote three days to the selection of candidates from two or three groups and use ingenious gym games devised by psychologists to test leadership, persuasiveness, reasoning ability under stress, initiative, ingenuity, physical fitness, dexterity, and team work. There are, no doubt, too many medical applicants to make it possible to apply such methods to all candidates. Headmasters' reports are sadly less reliable than they should be as a means of whittling down the numbers. Too many of them are liable to terminological inexactitudes in attempting to make their geese into swans. Some of them candidly do not know their pupils well enough to be able to attempt an answer to detailed questions about somewhat nebulous characteristics. Medical schools trying methods other than pure marks are laying themselves open to charges of 'old-boy net' or 'subjectivity'. Short interviews by inexperienced interviewers can be misleading. But I would be astonished if a small panel of experienced doctors and a headmaster, helped by a more detailed report and witnessing group discussions or individual problem solving, could not make a better job of picking the doctors of the future than those who rely exclusively on A level grades.

I believe that deans of admission should press the examination boards to make the special papers, on which distinctions and merits are assessed, more appropriate for medical selection and more quickly responsive to changing requirements. They should test problem solving, clear thinking, and powers of expression, and place much less stress on the accumulation of the kind of information demanded by the plain A level papers, which textbooks and computers can usually provide. These S papers are already a better guide than A grades and could, under medical advice, become more so.

A high proportion of injustices seem to me to arise from a lack of care in investigating the age at which advances are made and examinations are taken. Girls mature earlier than boys: they are often more emotionally balanced and mature at 17 or 18 and are capable of long, well presented essays, full of facts. On the other hand, they often seem to be less good at marshalling arguments and selecting the most relevant facts when competing against the clock. Furthermore there is one kind of adolescent mind which can be spectacularly successful at 13 or 14, but loses its edge in the early 20s. It is usually a mind with a youthful ability to memorise either pictorially or by sound and is accordingly capable of excelling at the still largely factual examinations at O and A level. This faculty can fade surprisingly quickly, and is not always replaced by the ability to ask oneself the right questions in the right sequence, which is more useful for an honours degree.

Headmasters are generally recognising that there are many children who do much better if they are not pushed ahead to take A levels at 16 or just 17. The clever 13-year-olds who were formerly accelerated to reach the 6th form at barely 15, arrived there too early and too immature to score well at A level. A high proportion of boys, who at 15, in full spots and confusion, appear to be of only average standard, 'shoot' after adolescence at 17 and 18. These are often the ones that do best at university. Especially those boys who grow to be very tall, going from 5ft 6 ins. to 6 ft 4 ins. between 13 and 16 do not realise their full academic (or physical) potential until they have grown into themselves. Also a number of children do not begin to realise their potential until they have made up their minds about their career..

For these reasons it is of the greatest importance that university selectors should not over-estimate the importance of O level grades, and even more important that headmasters should stress these kinds of factors in their reports.

Similarly the 'gap year' can be a decisive factor. While admitting that some high-grade mathematicians can 'go off the boil' if they do not keep going between leaving school and going up to university, I am sure that most boys and girls benefit from this interval before tackling more advanced work. Instead of wasting time celebrating their liberty by over-addiction to the social round as a change from academic work, they can get that out of their system far from home or university, get to know the world and return to work with an abiding interest in the whys and wherefores of death, sex, disease, poverty, brutality, love, and hate. This can lift their performance unrecognisably.

Finally I suspect that re-takers are under-estimated. A boy who has the guts to repeat his A level year is worth thinking about. He is often highly motivated.

Real scholars will continue to be needed. The cream of the cream will be recognisable even through A and S levels, especially if the special papers are further developed. But there is just as urgent a need for a rather different kind of quality among those who will not necessarily be the innovators and planners, but will be understanding, highly competent, dedicated, efficient people, prepared to work themselves to the bone for the happiness and well-being of their charges. To achieve this, selection procedures should be modified. The bonus may well be that many of the new selections will end by doing as well as or better than, even in purely academic terms, their precocious but less well balanced predecessors.

Diversification

Once upon a time, in the bad old days before and immediately after the war, British Heads worshipped the false idol of team games. Nearly all independent schools and a high proportion of state schools devoted the greater part of their pupils' time outside the classroom to compulsory football, cricket, rugby, hockey, lacrosse or netball. The best games players became prefects, and a blue was a safer route to Top Management than a First. The organisation was simple: everyone took exercise, and the maximum number of pupils were occupied in the most economical way. Fine for those with talents in that direction, but not for the rest.

Potential artists or poets spent ten or, in some schools, as much as 15 hours a week freezing in the deep field, as rough winds shook the darling buds of may, dropping catches and scoring ducks. As one cynical Head observed: 'Cricket is a great game for those who are good at it, but, like homosexuality, it is best practised in private between consenting adults.' In the winter, frail youngsters with a gift for the piano or a future as surgeons had their delicate fingers trampled in the scrum by larger and less sensitive boys, or miskicked the round ball to enable others to look skilled.

It made no sense, even to keen games players like myself. So, after the revolution of the sixties, we invented Diversification. The word was pretentious enough to attract liberal and intelligent parents and educationists, and it embodied a hopeful new approach.

It meant that schools would offer the widest possible variety of activities outside the classrooms. Pupils would choose what they enjoyed most and did best. The beauty of Diversification was that the net of opportunity would be cast so wide that even the tiniest talent would find a sphere for enthusiasm and success. New alternatives multiplied. In addition to football, rugby, cricket, hockey, lacrosse and netball, schools provided athletics, cross country, swimming, tennis, gymnastics, squash and badminton. Then it was dancing, cycling, basketball, golf, shooting and riding. Then orienteering, sailing, mountaineering, sail boarding, canoeing, social service and outdoor projects for geology, geography, biology and natural history. Finally there were indoor alternatives: drama, music, art and crafts, bridge, public speaking, chess or tiddleywinks.

Marvellous! That is how education should be. In a few well equipped, well placed, lucky or wealthy schools, Diversification more or less worked.

In many, however, it ran, and is still running into formidable snags.

Complete facilities cost a fortune. First class coaches are rare for any activity. Schools who could find four or five were lucky. Boys and girls of good sporting potential are thin on the ground. If a school has a dozen athletic youngsters and they are all playing football, at least there will be a good team and good competition. If they are divided between 12 different activities, the standard and the competition within each will be low. Schools offering both football and rugby did neither well.

If many of the better athletes didn't benefit by Diversification, the unathletic majority fared even worse. There is an unfortunate educational law: given free choice, the majority will go for the softest options. So the unathletic will opt for table tennis (which should be an athlete's game, but takes a short time), or tiddleywinks or nature rambles. By trying to offer everything, the school has ensured that nothing is well done.

Twenty years after Diversification, Britain has reached the stage when only independent schools with massive facilities and expensive coaches, or a few maintained schools lucky enough to be well provided and near large sports centres, are making a success of it. Over half over-16-year-olds have no organised exercise, and about the same proportion do not stir their stumps for the equivalent of a brisk two miles walk each week - less than is needed to give them a strong heart. There is only one compulsory P.E. period, and that is still a fiction in some schools. Football, rugby and cricket fields have been sold, and nothing has taken their place. T.V. watching is closing in on the abandoned time.

Diversification is right, no doubt about that. But it must be within limits. Schools can only offer activities for which they have time, good coaching and equipment, whether inside or outside the school. Non-classroom activities should be divided into sweaty and not sweaty, and every pupil should have a minimum of two sweaty activities per week. No ambitious pupil should be denied a chance to follow his or her ambition; but there should be firm guidance towards activities for which the rest are suited and for which there are good facilities. Everyone should have time for cultural hobbies as well as sweaty ones.

Time! There's the rub. It has been eaten away by the core curriculum and by the early closure of schools. For schools to finish at 3.30 when both parents are working until much later is foolish indulgence. A later closure could make available every afternoon a couple of hours for a whole range of sports activities, cultural hobbies and supervised homework which could transform our schools, make them more attractive and, by keeping unsupervised teenagers off the streets, go far towards transforming our society.

Prayer or Pill?

What has been the result of the great debate about co-education? How did it start?

Before and immediately after the war, it was hardly an issue. In most other countries it was accepted as a matter of course that human beings should be brought up together. In Britian the separatist tradition was strong, largely because so many of the brighter boys and girls went to boarding schools, and because few parents or teachers thought that there would be anything but disaster, under boarding conditions, unless the sexes were firmly isolated. The idea was deeply embedded in society that girls should study needlework, languages, music, art, history and biology (or, preferably, botany) and that they should face adolescence without the rough disturbance of pimply males, under the influence of mistresses who understood them and were unmoved by the fluttering of eyelashes or the ready use of tears.

Then came the Pill, the Rolling Stones and the Beatles. Things changed. Misguided parents abandoned their supervisory duties, gave up their homes to wild teenage parties and even installed snogging rooms. The difference between highly disciplined single-sex schools, holiday behaviour and permissive modern universities became untenable.

The thin end of the wedge came when independent school teachers, accustomed to having their sons educated free or cheaply at their own schools, began to send their daughters. Then there began to be pressure from parents to be allowed to send sisters to join their brothers because of geographic convenience. It began to be thought that, in a new world of career girls, there was much to be said for a shared curriculum, and that - at least in the sixth form - some experience of co-education in disciplined surroundings before the traumatic immersion in the freedom of university life was advisable. At the same time, some independent schools found that the demand for single-sex boarding schools was dropping. By taking bright girls from the single-sex girls' schools, they could keep up their academic standards.

So far so good. Unfortunately many schools had not thought it out clearly and rushed their fences. What should their policy be: barbed wire and machine guns, or prayer and the pill? How far should the sexes mix outside the classroom and what would the Heads do when John was, inevitably, found in bed with Jane - or, worse still, when Jane was found in bed with the rugby coach? In Germany teutonic thoroughness and lack of humour led to bizarre rules. The boys at Salem had rooms in the opposite wing of that splendid castle to the girls. If visits were made, the bed had to be trundled out into the corridor - presumably an echo of the British tradition that whatever is done should be done in the maximum of discomfort!

In the early days, when I was Chairman of the Eastern Heads, I saw mistakes were being made, conceitedly thought that I was not making too much of a mess of it all, and arranged a joint meeting of male and female independent school Heads in London - the first time that such a thing had ever been done.

I should have known better. We had disturbed a wasp's nest, and the ladies, led by the indomitable Miss Manners, laid into us with no holds barred. We were stealing their best girls, often without proper notice or consultation, thereby cutting their throats. We knew nothing about girls, who would wind us round their little fingers. Our coarse boys would corrupt them, they would be miserable, either isolated if ugly, or surrounded and knocked off balance if beautiful. We had not made proper preparations, had too few lady teachers, unsuitable accommodation. Above all, they maintained, girls would do better academically if left to the quiet and expertise of their own schools. We were sacrificing their standards in a vain effort to civilise our barbarians. What did we think we knew about women?

We 'ummed and 'ahed and did our best to put up some sort of a defence in an ineffectual Public School kind of way But, although they had exaggerated, the ladies certainly had made their views known, and if we had indeed known little about girls' schools and their Heads, we certainly learned a thing or two that day.

The early days were difficult and attended by frequent mistakes. Some schools undoubtedly 'poached' girls without proper notice. There were, initially, too few lady teachers. When there were only a dozen or a score girls in improvised accommodation, they did feel isolated. The charge that their academic performance would suffer if they were transferred into a co-ed school at the sixth form stage was not possible to prove; I can only say that of my first intake of 20, nineteen passed all their A levels and got university places, 5 at Oxbridge, with 3 open awards. Although any change of school demands a little settling time, it is hard to imagine that they could have done better. There were faults on the part of the girls' schools too. A former pupil of mine wanted to send his daughter to join his son at Gresham's. He gave plenty of notice, but the Headmistress told him that, although not without some academic ability, his daughter was quite unsuited to co-education. Father insisted. She came to us, got a fourth term scholarship to Oxbridge, and became an ideal Head Girl.

We had a little barbed wire and machine guns in the background. I was either lucky enough or negligent enough never to catch a couple in the act. Either they were clever or surprisingly virtuous. A little of both I suspect. I and my colleagues were not naïve enough to believe that love no longer laughs at locksmiths, but we believed in making it neither easy nor fashionable, and some of us succeeded.

I am convinced that sixth form co-education is a good thing, especially in a boarding school. It is probably a good thing all the way through, but I have less experience of this and am less sure.

My reasons are simple. It is important that the sexes should live and learn side by side, withour feeling that sex is the Great Unknown Desirable Sin. Complete separation at 16 and 17 leads to homosexuality, bullying, coarseness on the one hand and gigling and silliness on the other. When they are put together, manners improve and, provided clear guidelines are established, the dreaded prevalence of sexual intercourse seldom arises. And when and if it does, the formerly equally-dreaded pill ensures that it is without disastrous consequences. The girls are not lonely if they are given their own boarding houses with limited visiting hours. Hobbies like drama, music and art are greatly improved by avoiding, for instance, the need to have pretty 13-year-old boys mincing across the stage with unconcealably large feet and hands. The sexes compete, academic standards rise, everyone is happier and each learns from the other. Boys, being lazier and less mature, are nevertheless quicker to question and generally better at marshalling essential points in a logical order against the clock. What we always suspected is now proven. Girls are academically and in every way more mature at 15, less so, if at all, at 18. They are more conscientious, far better at understanding relationships and emotions, and much more sensitive to literature at a much earlier stage. Britain has always suffered more than most from being a nation in which 18-year-old males stand at one end of the room talking about games, while girls stand at the other and talk about, but seldom to, males. It even persists in middle age.

Given firm but reasonable discipline, plenty of lady teachers, good teaching, good accommodation and a huge array of games and hobbies, there is nothing to be said against co-education. One girl in 20 may feel isolated, but has the companionship of all her contemporary girls friends to choose from. One girl in 20 may have her head turned because she is greatly in demand, but it is surprising how rare this is. They are, in a good school, too busy mastering exciting new hobbies and rising to the top in class, to get into trouble.

Some girls may benefit from the peace and quiet of single-sex education during the difficult years 13-15; it is up to the parents to choose. And some boys may prefer the simple team values of an all male community. For my money, however, a good co-educational school provides the best education possible. The fact that some think it can all be done with love and kisses and no rules and discipline, and consequently fail disastrously, should not be allowed to take away from the great job being done by the majority.

The Old School Buy

Over 27 years at Gresham's I showed approximately 7,500 prospective parents around the school.

What changes over the years! In the 1950s prospective parents were mostly ex-public schoolboys or girls themselves. They didn't ask many questions, especially the mothers. If they were consulted by their husbands, it must have been well behind the scenes. Husbands assumed that nothing had changed, and that if something had been modified it would certainly be for the worse.

It's not like that now. Frank Fisher, when master of Wellington College, claimed that he was recently asked 25 searching questions by a prospective mum, who read them from her diary, listened attentively to the answers and put her children down for Repton.

Potential customers tend to look less far afield, apart from service families and those living abroad, because fares at beginning and end of term and at half-term add substantially to already high fees. Nevertheless, they are much more anxious to know exactly what they are buying. Much of the country's wealth lies in different hands. A higher proportion have not been to independent schools themselves. Mothers now seem to ask most of the questions and to make the decisions: they are less concerned with academic or sporting results, more interested in happiness, flexibility, humanity, comfort and liaison with home.

Unfortunately, Head teachers have had to respond by becoming salesmen for their schools - with the difference that they retain some power to facilitate or hinder ultimate entry. Peering out of my office window at the latest prospective parent car, I found myself forming silly prejudices. Quite unreasonably I warmed to large untidy estate cars or family saloons in preference to Rolls-Royces or Jaguars. It probably went back to the day when I was entertaining an old boy, who was also a high court judge, to tea. My seven-year-old daughter chose the moment we were discussing juvenile delinquency to escape naked from the nursery, to run out of the front door and to climb on to the roof of his Phantom 40/50, where she was clearly visible, energetically repulsing an embarrassed chauffeur's attempts to rescue his beautifully-polished car from her chocolate-sticky hands.

It wasn't easy to know what line to adopt. Some prospectives came because dad was a Rugby player who wished to have hell kicked out of his large son by an ex-rugby international headmaster.....one such actually reminded me that the last time he had seen me was when, as a second row forward for Richmond, he had caught me in a maul, twisted my neck and had been punched in the face in return. I suppose these things create bonds.

93

Others came because they had been told that Uppingham or Sedbergh might have been too tough for their sensitive and asthmatic little boy, and a prep school had thought that we might understand him better. Others came because of a particular strength of the school: maths science or squash.... The line appropriate for the parents of the asthmatic was quite unsuitable for the ex-rugby hearty.

I was not a good salesman; accidents were always happening. I took a particularly wealthy mum to watch the last five minutes of a school match on a cold December day - an idiotic idea. Her very powerful and expensive perfume, or the cold weather, strangely upset my wolfhound, normally an irreproachably courteous beast. To my horror, he lifted his leg without warning and performed (by no means half-heartedly) all over her new moon boots.

On another occasion a famous and successful old boy brought his French wife to look round. I had misread my appointments from my diary and, thinking that for once I had a free afternoon, had absconded to a local pike pond - successfully it transpired, for I caught a 14-pounder. My wife arrived with screeching brakes to inform me I was already half-an-hour late as I was struggling, blood-stained, fishified and mud-splattered, to remove my spinner from the pike's needle-sharp teeth. I was still wader-clad when I clattered back through my front door. He was remarkably forgiving, but her Parisian eyebrows shot up. Both boys were sent to Eton.

Yet smoothness and elegance do not always help. We had just completed new and attractive study bedrooms. I asked a wealthy oriental parent whether he would like to see them. 'No, Mr Bruce Lockhart, I would not! You must understand that in Hongkong my boys are very spoiled. They have a television set in every room, and a car is always at their disposal. I am sending them to England so that they can sleep in an uncomfortable bed in a cold old English dormitory like other boys!'

You cannot please all of the people all of the time.

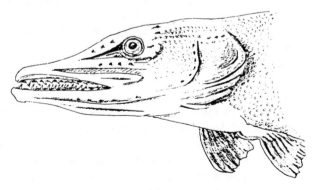

Education 2

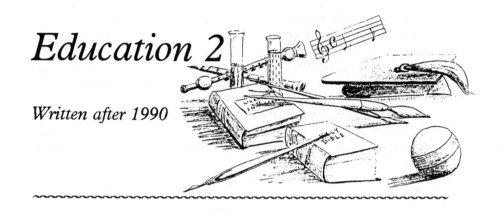

Written after 1990

The Heart of the Matter

Education, expected to be a major election issue, fell flat. Both big parties spent so much time attacking largely fictitious versions of their opponents' economic schemes, or imagined privatisation of the N.H.S., that education has been neglected.

The Conservatives are proud of their regular testing and of maintaining GCSE and A level standards, and of an old-fashioned emphasis on the three Rs. The Labour party promised to spend on training and to substitute flexibility for the core curriculum, and it had a last minute repentance about its intention to review the charitable status of independent schools. Paddy Ashdown promised a billion pounds for education without very precise or radical reforms. Both he and Labour want to end the assisted places scheme.

None of this tackles the heart of the matter. Britain looks after its bright pupils well. Only 19% of our girls and 18% of our boys get two A levels or better, and 25% of those come from 5% of independent schools. Only 12% of boys and 15% of girls get five C grade GCSEs or better. Those who need a fundamentally new approach are the 40% of boys and 33% of girls who get no GCSE C grades or better.

The most frightening and significant aspect of English education is that less than 40% stay on in full-time education after 16, even less if you confine the figure to secondary schools. This compares with 73% in Denmark, 69% in France, 49% in Germany, 77% in the Netherlands, 50% in Australia, 75% in

Canada, 77% in Japan, 71% in Sweden and 80% in the United States.

Admittedly we have a higher proportion of 16 to 18-year-olds in part-time education. But even counting all those in part-time education, Germany, Sweden, Japan, Canada and the Netherlands are still 20% ahead of us. We are well behind Scotland, which sends a 2½ times greater percentage of its school leavers to take degrees in science and technology.

This is not just a question of a little more money to be spent on training schemes. Our real target should be to get 90% staying on at school or in full-time education between 16 and 18. We should at once adopt a Five Higher Certificate approach modelled on the Scottish practice and closer to the rest of Europe. Careers and training must be devised which will be attractive enough to make pupils want to stay on at schools or colleges, practical enough to lead to a wide choice of careers, modern and technical enough to fit them for 21st century life and varied enough to make them human beings and not mere career fodder.

To offer a pale reflection of core curriculum subjects tailored for the top third is not enough. The bottom 40% must be offered not GCSE grades D and E, but courses at which they can excel, leading to skilled jobs at the top end, to jobs requiring competence in the middle, and rewarding work even for those near the bottom of the pile. Sweden, for instance, offers a special course with a special staffing ratio for their bottom 10% - and a careers advisory service which helps them with devoted care to find employment.

Courses for the bottom 40% must be set up by intensive liaison between business, industry and teachers. They must provide entry to in-service training later, with ladders at every stage to more advanced courses. Above all it must be recognised by 16-year-olds that further education is going to bring them financial reward, which would not be theirs if they were to leave school at 16.

This is our country's greatest need if we are to have a skilled workforce, low unemployment, and a huge reduction in the army of unqualified teenagers embarking on a parasitical life of street crime. Dreams of a classless society mean nothing until this is put right. It will need new subjects, new schools, new exams, new courses and new attitudes towards self-improvement among the working classes. It means a complete switching of our priorities from the top to the bottom. We will have to spend as high a proportion of GNP on education as other civilised nations.

If a bold solution to these problems figured in the manifesto of any of the three parties, I must have overlooked it.

Beware of the Weed by the Window

Be careful, ebullient and self-confident young teachers, to avoid the tempting mistake of treating pupils as if they were idiots. Most of them are, of course: it is the biggest shock to teachers embarking on their careers to discover that most pupils, even in quite good schools, don't learn anything until they have been told it ten times. We forget that we were no better.

Teachers would, nevertheless, be well-advised to remember that teenagers can be dynamite. It is not now that is the trouble, you can learn to deal with that. The fuse may be 20 or 30 years long. You may treat 20 spotty-faced adolescents with cheerful abandon as clots to be encouraged, bullied, mocked, jollied, urged and pushed to a slightly less sordid level - but pause before you show off your satirical wit at their expense.

Who is sitting in the back row, noting your weaknesses, your mistakes, your failings and your eccentricities? No peculiarity of speech, extravagance of gesture or disruptability of habit will go unmarked. That bespectacled weed nearest to the window may have scored only 7 out of 20 in his prep, but who or what is he; and especially who or what is he going to be?

We all hope that some record of our doings may survive; not all of us would choose for ourselves immortality through the sharp and critical eyes of a condescendingly-treated and grossly under-estimated future novelist. Little did I expect, when teaching as a conceited and over confident 30-year-old, that one of the apparently undistinguished pupils at the back of my class would one day be famous as the co-author of *If*, a film which portrayed, with riotous humour and vivid fantasy, the multitudinous weaknesses of a public school in the early 1950s. It ended, you may remember, in a meeting, and in the machine-gunning of the head, governors and staff on speech day. I don't think I recognised myself, but I'm not quite sure.

At various times I have held forth on subjects about which I knew comparatively little to young people of unsuspected and as yet under-developed brilliance. I have waffled about theology to future bishops, presumed to teach future Oxbridge choral scholars how to sing, told Colin Cowdrey how to do a late cut. I have taught French to Freddy Forsyth, taught ethics to someone subsequently imprisoned for murder, and held forth about literature to future writers of film scripts, musicals, poetry and satire. I must often have made myself utterly ridiculous.

Teachers' unguarded quips or *faux pas* are not so swiftly forgotten as the rule for the agreement of the past participle. The young may forget what they are supposed to learn from you, but their memory for your foibles is impeccable. The peculiar genius of adolescence lies in the clarity of its

97

perception of the oddities of adults. If you pick your nose, extract wax from your ears, shoot a line, clear your throat, raise your eyebrows, turn up in unusual clothing or do anything in a faintly caricaturable manner, you stand every chance of having it recorded for the delectation of all your other former pupils, your colleagues, your friends, your wife and children and grandchildren for years to come.

Never mind! The consolation is that teenagers generally like eccentrics. It is not the strongly individual teachers who tend to come out worst when the unhappy, supersensitive pupils of today write their disillusioned and fiercely critical autobiographies in the years to come.

Teachers can only do their best to treat them honestly and on the level, and with equal fairness. If they still want to make fun of you, so be it; let them enjoy themselves. If you find yourself criticised in a best-seller 20 years later, don't make a fuss, just take a leaf from the Duke of Wellington who told an indiscreet lady friend to 'Publish and be damned.'

Catch the Rebels Young

Any teacher over 45 referring to the Revolution is likely to be talking not of Oliver Cromwell or the guillotine, but of the student revolution at the end of the sixties.

It was dramatic. One term, lots of neatly turned-out pupils volunteered to come every day after lunch to the head's private rooms to listen with rapt attention to Mozart, Bach or Schubert. The next they became abruptly long-haired and scruffy, stomped up and down in their studies to the Big Beat, volunteered for nothing, grumbled about everything and became spotty, discourteous and sullen.

Teachers were perplexed. They all thought they had lost their grip. As usual when things go wrong, they blamed the equally-puzzled parents. At home, previously contented and obedient children suddenly clamoured for more pocket money to follow teenage fashion. Little 13-year-olds wanted to go to disreputable discos in private houses where the absence of adults was a requisite. Help with the washing up and tidying of rooms gave way to late rising and endless pop music.

A headmaster colleague sent for one of the most idle and tiresome of that generation. 'You're not doing any serious work this term, Robinson.... I really don't know what you're going to do in the Great World Outside'.

'Oh don't worry about that, sir! You see, it isn't your kind of world any more!'

98

He was right and wrong. After nearly 25 years of trying to sort it all out, we still have not entirely succeeded. The children of the Revolution can still be identified by their whole attitude to the world. Society is the enemy which owes them everything; their duties and debts to society are nil. They are marked by eternal ingratitude.

Teachers and parents, weary after the war, had dreamed of a return to an unchanging peace which had never been. Wanting no more upheavals, they stuck their heads in the sand, refusing to face the huge new problems which were to make life change more quickly than ever before: the Bomb, the Pill, drugs, computers, Women's Lib, cheap travel, swift communications, race relations and rejection of authority.

It was good that these things should be faced, that the unthinking relegation of women to the kitchen sink should be challenged, that homosexuals and lesbians should no longer be mercilessly persecuted, that illegitimate children should not be disgraced and condemned for their whole lives, that weapons of mass destruction should be feared and their use questioned.

It was good that we should have to listen to the young, to adapt to a technological world and to make teaching more entertaining, making pupils watch and do instead of just listen. But terrible mistakes were made. Teachers and parents lost confidence and respect, abandoning the good with the bad.

Many could no longer believe in traditional christianity - and then found that they had no strong spiritual or moral values to put in its place. Child-centred education. instead of meaning that teachers and parents should start by considering what was best for every child, came to stand for 'do as you please'. 'All lifestyles are equally valid' became a progressive slogan which did irreparable harm. Theorists criticised any attempt at moral leadership as authoritarianism or paternalism. In some circles classroom discipline was condemned, punishment virtually abandoned, bad manners and bad language tolerated, homework almost given up, games and hobbies largely renounced.

Parents no longer worked or played with their children and school finished earlier and earlier. The result was that schools offered little challenge. Children were often unsupervised for two or three hours between the end of school and the return of their parents from work. When they eventually returned, tired parents handed bored children over to the television and gave them too much pocket money. The proportion of children staying at school after 16 was - and still is - the lowest among western democracies.

Bored stiff, unqualified and almost unemployable, a large underclass of teenagers developed. Inevitably many of them (see Manchester University's recent research) turned to drugs. Their only other excitement was to swell the wave of crime and violence, or to put citizens at risk by incompetent driving of stolen cars. Employment is hard enough to find for the able and willing: for this underclass it is almost impossible.

The Tory conference on law and order spent most of its time discussing more and longer prison sentences. The heart of the matter lies in our homes and schools. John Major would do better to focus his efforts on this much earlier and more relevant stage - and thus to empty prisons, not fill them.

Tales of the Unexpected

One of the most stimulating features of a boarding school teacher's life is that anything may happen at any time.

Adolescence is a time of precarious balance, and if thousands of adolescents pass through your school, you will see the whole range of possible human behaviour. My grandfather, father and brother and I were all boarding school Heads, for a total time of nearly a century. Between us we experienced everything from the tragic and gruesome to the hilarious. Some of the incidents like suicide, madness or attempted murder, or the 6 a.m. telephone call to tell me there was a body in my swimming bath, were hardly material for light-hearted reminiscences.

Fortunately many of the incidents were of the kind that may be revealed in retirement, and not many involved the law. Just as well, for I learned as a young man that a headmaster's relationship with the law can be delicate.

A long time ago, a pupil, already in trouble for misdemeanours within the school, overstepped the mark. He found a flash car in a London street while on holiday, drove it back to Norfolk and hid it in a friend's barn. He was later caught by the police. I decided he must be expelled, and posted a notice to this effect.

When the case came up, the second master attended to see fair play. He did so well that the boy got off, on the grounds, I believe, that it was a first offence, and that there was 'intent to return'. Father thereupon wrote demanding that I should take his boy back, as he had been cleared by British justice. This I declined to do, although I undertook to report to my governors that he was not expelled for theft, but for borrowing a car with intent to return.

I told the whole story to my governors later, very rashly concluding with the words: 'I'm afraid, gentlemen, that the law is sometimes an ass!' After the meeting a senior governor came up came up to me quietly and said: 'I think, Logie, that you should know that I was the magistrate in charge of the case!'

Adolescents are curious and, therefore, liable to experiment outside normal spheres. One evening, I was working late in my study, when the house captain came in and said: 'Sir, something really rather worrying has happened. We've put S.......... away!' I rushed through to S's study. T........., a scholarly and usually irreproachable Scot, was looking down at S, who, pale and breathing slowly and deeply, was slumped unconscious over his desk. It transpired that they had been reading a book on hypnosis. It had worked spectacularly, but the book did not say how the trance should be ended.

He was far gone. I carried him to my study and called the doctor, who was out. Was I to say in incantatory tones: 'I shall count back from ten to zero....on the count of zero you will wake up refreshed!' - or not? Not! He eventually came round before the doctor arrived. T appropriately got a science scholarship to Cambridge, S entered holy orders.

Where there are adolescents there are practical jokes. A pupil of unusual background once took the anatomy department's skeleton, dressed it in a gown and mortarboard, and seated it at the chapel organ before morning prayers. The director of music must have had quite a shock when he came in to play the voluntary. The chaplain felt that there was some degree of sacrilege, and the biologists were not amused by the possible damage to their expensive skeleton.

Similarly a few farmers' sons decided that it would be fun to carry a large sheep up to the staff common room in the early morning before the end-of-term meeting. As the sheep appeared to be house-trained, neither caused nor suffered damage, and was returned safely to its owner, it did not seem a major crime - but a line must be drawn. Such matters are not the least interesting aspects of school life

A Little Redtime Reading

Twenty-five years ago, Soren Jansen and Jasper Jensen launched the original little red schoolbook in Denmark. It was later translated into English by Berit Thornberry and adapted for Britain by 'Alan, Elizabeth, Hilary, Richard, Roger and Ruth'.

Times change and even the most fossilised among us change with them. Who remembers the little red schoolbook now? Yet it created a stir, raised headmasters' blood pressures and is a fascinating record of the days of the student revolution. It was more the product of those ideas than it was their instigator, but it had some of the same power and simplicity that Marx and Engels found in their Communist Manifesto, before the Old Prophet wrote that ponderous and indigestible *Das Kapital*.

I don't know how many pupils read it, but the heads certainly did. At the time we seethed. The passage of time has made a lot of the purely educational ideas seem acceptable. The writers have a permissive, but not unhelpful line on sex and are positively old-fashioned in their opposition to drugs, even cannabis. 'You are free to accept drugs or not. If you accept, you lose part of your freedom. Afterwards you're not free, the drug rules your life.'

Their idea of a good school goes no further, of course, than A. S. Neill's Summerhill. What pleases the pupils is good; what pleases the authorities is bad, because it is inspired by class-consciousness, lust for power and fear of change - and also, in some mysterious, never-defined way, by Big Business. Yet they had a few good ideas which helped to change attitudes. Teachers should listen to their pupils; should devote more care and skill to those who had the greatest learning difficulties; and should seek to develop talents more varied and practical than traditional academic subjects. The authors demanded more questioning and more participation and campaigned for school councils - even if they were disappointed when the councils asked for more homework instead of just more freedom.

They were right to suggest that classrooms, corridors and playgrounds should be brightened up. They recommended that teachers should be given experience of the wider world by sabbatical years, and that pupils in their last year should also be given experience of work outside school. They championed better careers advice, which was desperately badly needed, and they opposed excessive early specialisation. They were unexpectedly perceptive about pornography. 'Okay if not taken seriously or believed to be real life. Anyone who mistakes it for real life will be greatly disappointed.' Finally they took up the cause of girls, calling for an end to discrimination.

Unfortunately that was only the icing on a fundamentally sour cake. Marxist class-consciousness pervades all their thinking, and as you read further in the book, you begin to see how distorted and political it is. Marks are a swindle and exams a menace, because they indicate falsely that some are better and more deserving than others on the basis of middle-class academic criteria. For teachers to seek to impose 'good manners or speaking posh' is an attempt to force foreign culture on the working-class.

Class teaching is wrong. You must be allowed to work in your own way. Streaming is always wrong because it reinforces class differences. 'Discipline is only imposed out of fear.' 'Teachers expect children with working-class accents or immigrant backgrounds to learn less and therefore teach them less.' (Many of us found new arrivals to be much more teachable and hard-working than home-grown pupils!) Teachers are there to teach you to obey authority rather than question things, just as exams encourage you to conform and not be individual. (Lord how we hoped and searched for a trace of real individual and self-questioning!) 'Teachers think that people should have to do boring things as well as what interests them, because then they will learn that there is something called duty and that they will have to obey orders and do boring things later in life.'

There's the rub. Duty is the enemy and unconditional rights the aim. We gradually see what is 'boring' and 'interesting'. Art, woodwork and cookery are recommended instead of maths, reading and writing. If your class bores you and your teacher is traditional, pass notes, play the radio, discuss what interests you and write essays on your school and how it should be run. Arrange the desks in a circle.

The remainder of the book is a lesson in how to achieve pupil power and a lesson in revolution technique. There are detailed instructions on how to get rid of bad (i.e. traditional) teachers; how to get out of classes on religious education; how to use official and unofficial school magazines; and how to use banners, wall newspapers, slogans, demonstrations and strikes. It teaches the use of solidarity and tells pupils how to enlist parents' and teachers' support. Addresses are given of organisations which would help to spread the changes: the anti-corporal punishment organisation STOPP; the Schools Action Union; the National Council for Civil Liberties etc. Instructions are written in detail for complaining to or about heads, local education authorities, governors, the press and the B.B.C. There is advice on how to sabotage marks and examinations. Pupils are warned against joining teacher-organised societies. 'Are they trying to control you? Make you good citizens? If so, organise guitar-making and folk-singing instead.'

Finally, in case the reader is in any doubt, there is a wide and enlightened reading list: Fidel Castro - major speeches; Che Guevara - *Socialism and Man in Cuba*; Amilcar Cabrai - *Revolution in Guinea*.

Twenty-five years later we can wish the little red schoolbook happy birthday, secure in the knowledge that we have learnt as much from its bad side as from its good. It contributed to one disastrous change: the idea that everyone should insist on rights and privileges regardless of any duty to earn them by contributing to the general good. For that it should not be forgiven. It was also an exaggeration to assume that pupils are always divinely right and teachers wrong: the results have not proved invariably beneficial.

Otherwise it makes a charming and sometimes illuminating historical read, and much of its thinking has gained the widest acceptance - yet it is now as out of date as the generation it attacked, absorbed and neutered by the eternal British gift for compromise.

Quarts in Pint Pots

How do I fit it all into the time available, and, when I cannot, what do I do? This is every educationist's most important problem.

For many years the starting point was divinity, followed by English, mathematics, science, history, geography, a foreign language, art and music, physical education and sport. That became increasingly impossible as the post-war explosion of knowledge accelerated.

Science grew so that physics, chemistry and biology clamoured for time. Economics had to be taken seriously; computer studies became a necessity. Art began to expend into graphic design, computer work and new material crafts. Technology demanded more and more time. Social studies, sex education, dance and movement, drama, business studies and sports studies all staked a claim.

What could be done? There was a hunt for old-fashioned subjects to be thrown out. Greek and Latin were the first to go, followed by a second modern language for the bright and a single modern language for the less able.

Could physics, chemistry and biology be compressed into physical sciences or general science? They often were, and the gap between GCSE general science and individual sciences at A level became too big for most pupils to bridge. Could history and geography be compressed into something 'modern' and 'relevant' and renamed social studies? It was done in many schools. But, while pupils learnt to count television aerials and draw political conclusions from the results, they no longer knew what happened when, or where countries were.

Even then Heads found there was not enough room for the new subjects, so their eyes fell on religious studies, P.E. and sport, music and art. Religious studies dropped first to one period a week, then fell victim to the notion that to teach Christianity was 'indoctrination'.

P.E.? An excellent report was produced 18 months ago indicating what skills should be taught at what ages. Unfortunately the gap between the aims of the P.E. teachers and what is happening remains vast.

Music and art? Refuge was taken behind the erroneous theory that most children are tone deaf and have nothing to gain from music teaching. Art could be encouraged in the Plasticine years, but as soon as discipline was needed, it was left to a minority. Parents did not press for art - there did not seem to be much money in it.

That darling of the progressives, Jean Jacques Rousseau, said many things that should not be applied to mass education. In one respect, however, he was right. He said educators should seek to train the heart, the body, the imagination and the mind - in that order. For, if the heart be bad. a clever man will merely do more harm than a stupid one. If the body is unhealthy, its owner may lack the vigour to think or to act boldly. If the imagination is starved of art and music, the mind will lack power, delicacy, and the priceless vision of beauty.

Perhaps we should restore those most important sides of education to the centre of our school programmes - and then worry how to accommodate the other subjects to those who have talent for them. To do that, homework, in spite of the television, must be restored to pride of place.

In Praise of the Carrot and the Stick

A small boy is caught shoplifting: an everyday occurrence. The theft is trifling; even Blimps understand that it is not the end of the world. Most of us have at some stage taken some small thing belonging to someone else. We weren't hanged, neither did the law cut off our hand; but if we were caught, our parents, our teachers or the village bobby, or all of them, did their best to see that it didn't happen again. The modern response, however, is to do nothing, with the result that little groups of hardened children pinch to their hearts' content and soon become a serious menace.

It seems that no one can act against it. The shopkeeper often hesitates to stop a boy and search his pockets or satchel. If he uses force, or chases the boy and finds nothing, he may be in serious trouble. If the boy is with his parents, the parents will support their child whatever the facts. Even if the matter is clear and if he reports it to a policeman, the policeman is helpless.

If the policeman shouts at the boy or uses any force, he may be accused of assault. If he takes the lad home and tries to tell his parents what he has been doing, the odds are that he will be sworn at for making accusations without witness or proof, and the door will be slammed in his face. If he takes him to his head teacher, the Head will be so submerged in all the difficulties of discipline within the school that he may refuse to take any responsibility for a crime committed outside, when the boy should have been under the control of his parents.

There is no point in taking the boy to the police station and giving him a fright by threatening to bring him up before the magistrates. The boy knows perfectly well that he is too young to be sentenced in a magistrates' court. Only older children who are proving repeated offenders can be brought to book for such sins.Perhaps the social services will help? Not likely. Their recommendation is that above all voices should not be raised in anger, nor punishments inflicted. Parents must explain that shoplifting is wrong, but on no account should they make too much of it, or they may cause an unexpected reaction.

Corporal punishment is on the way out. To run a home or school without corporal punishment is admirable; but its absence can only work well in schools or homes with strong-minded teachers and good parents - and when ingenious systems of punishments and rewards have been evolved to take its place.

Punishments like service duties, extra work, loss of half holidays or loss of privileges have almost disappeared from our schools. No stick and, alas, no carrots either. Stars for effort, merit marks for good work, distinctions, prizes, special rewards and privileges have been widely rejected as part of the misguided campaign against competition.

Honest bribery works. One boy at school A is full of enthusiasm. Though not particularly bright, he works for his stars, his merits and his prizes for effort. He is proud of his good marks and concerned about his black marks. His parents are constantly informed when he is doing well and when he is failing.

His brother at school B appeared to be doing little homework. When, at last, some was found, it was disorganised, illiterate and ill-informed. Corrections were minimal. When dad approached his teachers, he was told: 'I don't know why you're worried, he's doing fine.' No incentives, no punishments, very little awareness of how poor his progress was. The boy was therefore bored and without ambition.

There is a deep-rooted fear of competition. Yet the world is harsh and competitive, and other countries recognise the fact. The English have a complex about not creating an élite, and believe that any creation of an order of merit damages the unsuccessful by giving them a sense of failure. A London head was quoted as saying : 'The trouble with these Asians is that their parents all want them to become lawyers and doctors.' Another said to a parent who had complained about shortage of homework: 'You should not pitch your expectations too high, we cater for very humble ambitions here.' It is a pity the English don't follow the Asian example.

It is nonsense to suppose that carrot and stick systems do not do better for all levels of children. Children enjoy competition, provided the slowest are not set

106

against the brightest, and provided effort and non-academic gifts are recognised as well as sheer achievement. Elites are a splendid thing as long as they include élites of helpfulness, craftsmanship, games, good manners, artistic sense and effort.

Utopia may afford to do without metaphorical sticks and carrots, but modern Britain needs them desperately, before people start to take the law into their own hands.

Bumf

After 37 years of teaching in independent boarding schools, and with three children teaching in state comprehensives, how familiar is the resentment against teachers' so-called privilege, long holidays and short working hours.

Most boarding school teachers used to start by attending prayers and assembly at 8.45 every morning. They taught 30 periods per week, coached games, supervised swimming, organised hobbies, took biology projects or held play or music rehearsals every afternoon. They taught again until 6 p.m., then interviewed pupils, took tutorial groups, presided at debates, took part in common room or committee meetings, the countless society activities, or supervised the two hours of homework.

Those who were house tutors or house masters or mistresses took evening prayers at 8.45 and then dealt with the queue of pupils with individual problems. They could seldom start corrections, preparation of lessons or setting of examinations until the late evening.

On Saturdays it was work as usual until lunch, and then most would either entertain visiting teams or referee a match - generally both. Or they would travel away with other groups for matches or for cultural expeditions. Even on Sundays there were religious services to attend, activities in which to participate, supervisory responsibilities - no question of overtime.

Holidays were long. But many staff devoted a large part of them to taking school expeditions, to organising camps, conferences or refresher courses. Others would seek to pay for their games equipment or give private tuition or mark examinations. Most had to work to update their knowledge.

In between there was the administration, liaison with parents, careers and university advice, disciplinary problems, responsibility for food and health, the finances of the various societies and the strain of the inevitable periodic crises.

It was excessive. Wives and children suffered, and there are limits to endurance. Yet most teachers were not unhappy. Whether hard work is acceptable or unacceptable is not primarily a matter of hours, nor even a matter of pay. Hard work can be fun if it is getting you where you want to go, if it is getting results and doing good, if it is challenging your skill and imagination and, above all, if it is appreciated.

What is causing the present unrest is not so much the hard work, but the futility of superfluous bureaucratic work which has made so many professional jobs increasingly unrewarding in the last couple of decades.

John Patten does not understand the teachers' world. Top teachers are not consulted or considered. They are emphatically not appreciated. You have only to hear him speak to recognise the repeated wrong notes and to feel the hackles rise.

Yes, standards do need a boost. Yes, a more flexible core curriculum is needed. Yes, good teachers should be paid better than bad. Yes, progress should be monitored, and exams are essential. It could all be done better and differently with tact and consultation. Progress at 14 could be monitored by ensuring that schools themselves tested regularly, and by monitoring a few sample pupils from top, middle and bottom. The Department of Education and Science should not get involved with choosing between Trollope and Henry Fielding, or between 'progressive' and 'traditional' methods. There are brilliant teachers of each persuasion, and even more who combine both.

Resentment is caused by unproductive work. I remember at the busiest time of year, while answering over 50 letters a day, receiving a request to return to the D.E.S. a list of all the rooms in my school, with the cubic footage of each. There were about 2,000 rooms from a photographic dark-room to a chapel!

No wonder teachers do not love their D.E.S.!

League Tables

It has been the silly season again. Competition is fine, and the government is right to insist that full details of examination results should be available. What is wrong is the attempt to produce an order of merit.

It is wrong because it seems to be impossible to avoid mistakes serious enough to make a farce of the whole league. It is wrong because it takes no account of different policies in different schools with regard to the age at which exams are taken. The chairman of the Headmasters' Conference and the headmaster of Langley both wrote to point out how ridiculous it is to base the number of GCSE candidates on the number of pupils aged 15 at the start of the school year. Many pupils are too old or too young to be included, and those aged 15 not in the fifth form and not taking exams are recorded as failures. Langley's score was reduced from 63% tp 52%, Gresham's from 98% to 83%.

'I feel sorry,' wrote the chairman, 'for the boy whose 10 A grades simply didn't count, and for the many schools with an impeccable 100% GCSEs A-C who appear with outcomes of 80%.

That in itself makes the order of merit a travesty; but there are many more anomalies. A school admitting girls to its sixth form whose 16th birthday is after September 1 has to add them to the number of its GCSE candidates, although the results (correctly) are added to those of the previous school.

Things are no better at A level. In the better schools many of the brightest pupils are entered for a single A level (for instance in maths or chemistry) after one year to free them for three A levels after two years. The score for this A level is not credited to the 'average university score'. It can only be discovered by looking under the 'single A level score' published later, when a discerning eye can spot the average of 7 or 8 amongst the 2s and 3s. The result is, the more bright double A level maths candidates you have, the lower your score.

It is also grotesque to compare the results of very small schools with a handful of GCSE candidates to those of big schools with hundreds. Even a civil servant should have been alerted to the pleasant little school, Casterton, placed above Winchester. The same kind of mistake has distorted the lists this year.

The proportion of pupils gaining five GCSEs A-C is useless as a guide to high scholarship or even merely to competence, unless it is related to the IQ of the candidates embarking on the course.

The leagues are not only misleading, they are dangerous. An ambitious head - and most are ambitious - can improve his or her results by doing things which are educationally undesirable. I remember one Yorkshire head saying: 'If my parents want me to produce boys with hairy legs and A levels in African dialects, hairy legs and African dialects are what I shall produce!'

So if you want to be top of the leagues, here's some advice.

Only let your pupils sit for their best GCSE subjects so that they can concentrate on six instead of 9 or 10 subjects.

Get rid of pupils who look as if they might score D grades only.

Don't allow anyone into your sixth form who might only pass A levels at humble grade, however promising he or she might be in other ways.

Encourage all your examination candidates to give up music, art, drama, sport, social service and hobbies.

You might rise to the top of the leagues, but you may be sure you would be running a worse school. The true measure of a school, even in purely academic terms, is how many A grades it obtains for its able pupils and how many pass grades it obtains for border-line candidates of shaky ability. The leagues give no clear guidance on either of these matters. If you want to know, go and get the complete results from those schools in which you are interested, and draw your own conclusions.

Provence

Butterflies and Bach

Roll on, golden Monday! The warm, but not yet burning sun caresses my toes as I poke them gently out of bed. The intermittent nightmares about losing clothes, cars or children, which I experience at home, have given way to the cheerful and excessively conceited dreams induced by the lavender season and by the intoxicating scent from the banks of lemon-yellow broom behind the cabanon.

Last night my feat of rescuing an old lady from an upper floor window by brilliantly combining three ladders was jubilantly acclaimed by the villagers, and properly rewarded by my appointment as Prime Minister of France. In a second instalment, I was a benevolent Pirate King bestowing the fruits of my plunder from the rich on the grateful poor.

As I slip on my bathing trunks and carry the French bread, peaches and coffee to our table on the terrace, I spare a thought for my children in Britain, already battling their way to work through mist and rain. I lie cosily back in a deck chair contemplating the wild and dramatic view.

It might be the Western Highlands, were it not for the unfailing sun and the chattering cicadas. An eagle wheels overhead. It is Bach morning on the radio. As the inspired build up of a concerto reaches its climax with the frenzied continuo leading into that great rollicking tune - tum tum TUM tum, tiddle tiddle tiddle diddy, tum tum tum tum TUM tum -the butterflies on the lavender seem, through half-closed eyelids, to be fluttering in time to the music.

And what butterflies! Lime-coloured Cleopatra splashed with orange, the two-tailed pasha, swift as a swallow with his dark chocolate wings bordered in light red. A silver-washed fritillary and an adonis blue provide other gleams of colour, while humming bird hawk moths busily sip their honeyed way from spike to spike. The gentle hum of endless varieties of bees, wasps and hoverflies against the bass of the great blue-black carpenter bee with his scintillating violet wings threatens to lull me back to sleep.

I shall stay here for an hour. As I glance over at my bikini-clad wife, we discuss the latest Iris Murdoch, butterflies and the day's programme.

So this is retirement and old age which we so much dread! We know, of course, that the storms will break over everyone's head in the end; but in the meantime, what more could life offer?

More money? Instead of a primitive stone place supplied with water from big rain tanks, a villa with all mod cons and a swimming pool? Just so many more gadgets to worry about: we can swim all day in the lake anyway. Champagne and caviar and lobster instead of Marius' red wine at 4fr 50 a litre, pâté and peaches? Would be nice now and again, but I'm content. The *Times* every morning and the telly at night? Thank God, no! We can guess what the football hooligans are up to and how many children have been murdered and abused. Venice, Barbados, Tahiti? The sun is no warmer, the crowds tiresome and the hassle not worth it.

A Rolls, servants hovering with iced cocktails and money-grubbing flatterers hanging on every word? No , thanks. It might be nice to write a best-seller - acclaim, fame and enough cash to solve my children's problems - but that will have to wait until the weather's cooler, and my talent develops, probably therefore, for ever.

An occasional glimpse of high life might be fun, but think how quickly it turns to cirrhosis, worry-ulcers and, ultimately, boredom: look at the elderly rich and take thought.

Now that I've written this, the hour after the hour in the deck chair is over. There are hard decisions to make. A swim in the lake, a visit to an old friend to talk about the world in his swimming pool as the thermometer rises to 90? Photographing insects? Painting another slightly less bad picture?

I suppose I should be ashamed. After a life time of very hard work, a Puritan conscience about this lotus-eating existence always rattles around in the depths of my mind. It can't be right that I should enjoy life so selfishly when the world is so full of misery and poverty and in such need of help.

I always put off thinking about that until I get back to England. We are certainly unlikely to solve it on our return to the terrace over a 6 o'clock glass of wine, when the evening light is yet more entrancing and when we shall be back to Bach and butterflies instead of the 6 o'clock news......

No Beginner's Luck in Provence

To gild my Provençal heaven yet further, I have been given three toys: Zeiss field glasses, a super watercolour set with easel and all accessories, and a Japanese camera. What a wealth of fun and discovery lies ahead! Retired and with ample time, there is no excuse for failing to embark upon a whole new life. I am in one of the most beautiful landscapes in the world, surrounded by fascinating birds, animals, insects and flowers, just waiting for me to record them so that others may share in their loveliness.

Just one snag: my incurable incompetence. The field glasses I can manage. To twiddle two simple knurled rings until I can see clearly, lies within my technological limits; I can do it quite nimbly. Black dots in the blue sky obediently resolve themselves into goshawks, ravens, black kites or short-toed eagles. Nondescript forms flitting from bush to bush assume brilliant colours and elegant shapes.

Field glasses do not record, however. Is anything as absorbing as the struggle to capture light and atmosphere in watercolours? I do not ask to put the mountain sunset on paper: even Turner could not do it. I do not expect to wield my paint brushes as magic wands, to leave a message for posterity, or even to sell a painting to an unperceptive friend for 30 guineas. But I should like to paint a tree that was not a mockery of treehood, or a maquis-covered mountain in the evening light that conveyed a hint of the glorious reality. Unfortunately, when confronted with the need to express the beauty with which my eyes are surfeited in terms of carbon marks upon white paper and in fluid pigments, all is lost.

So I turn for consolation to the Japanese camera: three instruction books in five languages, a tripod, a selection of lenses, and a case. A highly-trained young biologist, whose natural history photography I have much admired, was delighted to explain how it works. He could hardly believe that anyone could have reached advanced middle age without ever having taken a photo, even with a Brownie. Tactfully concealing the fact that he plainly knew an ass when he saw one, he told me the camera had been chosen because you could not go wrong. Everything was automatic; should you be in danger of making a mistake, lights flashed on all sides. He launched into a detailed analysis of all parts and functions of the camera and of its accessories.

I understood it at the time. But by the time I had reached France, two hours were needed to re-read and re-understand the instructions enough to dare to take a photo with the ordinary lens at infinity on a sunny day. Soon afterwards I embarked on insects with zoom and telephoto lenses, and that is something else.

I was surrounded by opportunities such as every nature photographer must dream of. A goshawk flew straight over the hut. A gecko darted out when we were dining and caught a yellow underwing. A short-toed eagle hovered overhead and was dive-bombed (actually hit) by a sparrowhawk. A bee-eater settled in the olive tree nearest to my front door. An ocellated lizard, sparkling green, posed in front of a wall. Three different kinds of swallowtail, a painted lady, a two-tailed pasha and a hummingbird hawk moth display daily.

For a week I rushed to my camera case and raced to fit the right lens. Each time I was too slow - the lizard had disappeared or the bird flown. At last commonsense took over. I must shorten my aim and set myself a single task.

Butterflies: beautiful, abundant and not timid.

The swallowtails were fine. They fly slowly, they are tame, they bask open-winged on anticipatable flowers. Not so the two-tailed pasha. In my copy of the *Field Guide to European Butterflies*, he is the only one, through some strange oversight, whose wing is portrayed only from the underside. The upperside is described (a travesty of justice) as 'dark brown with a broad fulvous border'. Fulvous! Orange, at least. I was determined to capture the elusive upper wing.

The problem was not so much that the pasha was not tame. On the contrary, it appeared to conceive a strange passion for me. On the rare occasions it rested on its favourite stone or flower, it would clasp its wings firmly overhead, concealing the upper wing. As soon as it saw me, it hurtled off on a circular flight of 50 yards circumference at two to three times swallowtail speed, returning to me at head height and jinking, like a hedge-hopping Spitfire avoiding flak. Twice it landed on my camera, three times in my hair and once on my trigger finger. And on every occasion it fanned out its wings to show its full splendour.

That night I fell exhausted into bed. At about eleven o'clock I was rudely awoken. My wife was shaking me and whispering: 'Logie! Wake up! There's someone outside the door!'

Ours is not the sort of door people are outside. Half a mile of impossible track separates us from the nearest country road. But I could indeed hear footsteps crunching on the gravel. I grabbed a torch, flung open the door and stepped outside. There on the threshold, not two yards away, stood a large and astonished wild boar. It wheeled away (fortunately) and trotted down the track.

When about twenty yards away, it paused and turned to face me. He seemed very big, well tusked and peculiarly unfrightened, no doubt puzzled and dazzled by the torch. He trotted off, this time for good.

It occurred to me that I had not yet learned how to fit the flash equipment to my camera.

Post Haste in Provence

We grumble about the British post. Try a couple of months in Provence, and you will think the British Post Office the world's finest organisation.

Mark you, it's partly my fault. If I choose to live in a stone hut up a kilometre of track that makes the Old Glencoe road look like the M1, and try to keep in touch with base in Norfolk, I should expect difficulties. No doubt there are crofts in the Outer Hebrides where service is irregular. Nor is it a lack of local goodwill. The village postman greets us like long-lost friends; a chat with him is always a pleasure. Our letter box is nailed to an oak tree by the roadside where our track starts; it is one kilometre from my hut and three from the village post office. Shortly before the 12 to 5 siesta, the postman hangs about the square hoping to catch all the outlying villagers and country folk, either as they leave the one and only shop or as they have a 'pression' at the tables outside the one and only pub. With charming courtesy, as befits an old soldier, he doffs his official cap and exchanges gossip with each before delving in the depths of his bag to distribute the mail. 'Ah, Monsieur Bruce Lockhart! You could not save me a journey by taking a few letters for Mme Pitchou and Monsieur Estève?' Of course, with pleasure.

If we miss the village square for two or three days in succession, the postman's conscience pricks him and somehow the mail reaches the letter box. But recently there has been a problem. Not just the periodic absence of his false

114

teeth - that just makes his broad Midi accent a little harder to understand. It's his piles. They are not referred to; yet everyone in the village knows 'in confidence'. This painful affliction has made his journeys on bumpy country roads on an antedeluvian motor bike impossible. Under the circumstances his plans to decentralise the distribution of mail have become so complex that it is not surprising that things go wrong. Taking pity on him one day, I took him on his entire rounds in my car. It gave me some sympathy for his tactics. Not only were some tracks worse than mine, but each lonely house was guarded by half-starved mongrels with a touch of mastiff, alsatian and great Dane, which roared and rattled at their chains - or, worse still, didn't, and just leapt at the car.

Our letter-box shares the oak tree with two other egregious hermits. Although lockable, I suspect all local boxes respond to the same key. They are so small that only the smallest letters and children's hands can get inside. Substantial envelopes are clamped to the outside with a clothes peg, a technique used for the cheque for my golden bowler on retirement. Fortunately the honesty of the locals is as remarkable as their inefficiency.

Rustic arrangements do not play nearly so large a part in delays as some mysterious department of the bureaucracy further back. Apparently British post offices are not allowed to accept advance payment to ensure that proper stamps are put on mail to be redirected from Norfolk to Provence. So most of my mail, understamped, is held up for anything from a week to three weeks before delivery, although I would be delighted to pay cash on delivery or at the post office. Everyone loses by this arrangement. Even more mysterious is the manner in which bills and letters from the Inland Revenue get through within a week, while cheques and personal letters are interminably delayed.

It is hard to explain local conditions to H.M. Inspectors of Taxes. Mine sent a letter requesting a substantial payment by a date not many days away. I opened it with trembling fingers before getting into my car. No sooner had I glimpsed the figure than the Mistral, blowing at gale force, whisked the letter from my hand and blew it irretrievably into a jungle of brambles and gorse. My friendly letter of explanation, enclosing a cheque for what I could remember of the amount due to what I could remember of his address (I keep few files in Provence), is unlikely to secure prompt payment, or exemption from interest on an overdue debt.

This is not a place to recommend to freelance journalists wrestling with deadlines, or anxious to be up to date with the news. To re-establish home links, I am trying to have a telephone installed. It took three letters, two phone calls and six weeks before I got a reply, asking a large number of questions and telling me they would consider my application lapsed if I did not reply within

115

15 days. By the time this peremptory missive reached me (from 30 kilometres away) I had three days left. I'll be lucky, my friends tell me, if I get it within a year.

In the meantime my Norfolk telephone account was paid on the day of receipt - 18 days after it was posted. Nearly four weeks later I received the final demand posted a fortnight earlier. Presumably I am now cut off.

Never mind. The postman's piles may soon be better.

Perhaps Oldies Shouldn't Camp

When couples are growing old, they suffer from periodic wild impulses to recapture their youth: foolish jogging, cycle tours in France, second honeymoons, attempts to dance to rock music when you rock not, neither do you roll.

We camped a lot in the Highlands of Scotland and in the South of France in the days of long ago, when 'camping sauvage' was not a sin and youth and blood were warmer. Ageing memories are selective, forgetting midges and clegs and remembering the sunsets and the wine. Yet there were some flaws even then in the bliss of camping. There was the time when we returned after a ramble in Ardnamurchan to find a melancholy, unaggressive, shaggy Highland bull chewing a strip of canvas four feet long, neatly excised from the roof of our tent..... When one of our two accompanying children gave a piercing yell because his finger was stuck round the sharp edge of a half open, circular butter tin, which so startled his elder sister that she immediately spilt the boiling kettle over her legs.... When in a temperature of over 100 degrees in the Camargue, remembering the particularly vicious mosquitoes from a previous venture, we took to a caravan. We didn't dare to open a window, and the temperature rose so high that a nameless member of the family hurled an unloved guitar along the table in a fit of exasperation. It gathered pace and shot through the window. Every mosquito in the Camargue smelt blood and rushed in through the gap to feast on us...

These things happen over the years. They did not discourage my wife and myself from deciding, in the glorious May weather of Provence, to put up the tent, partly out of nostalgia, partly to create more room. The tent was one of those blue and orange atrocities, fortunately faded to gentler hues. It had an ante-chamber and an inner sanctum, supposedly insect-proof; it was nearly as old as us, and that's saying something.

Camping used to be easy. My elder son and I used to pull the two bags out of the car and perform a synchronised dance to the tune of Colonel Bogey, with world war two words attached. The tent would be up in four minutes; collapsed and packed away in three. Or so we remembered.

Unfortunately neither my wife nor I could remember the sequence. Dismantling and installing used to be done in the cool of morning and of evening. The end of May in Provence at midday is hot. Nothing fitted, everything was rusty. A crucial frame rod was missing. There were some spares - just of the wrong length. I began to feel sharp pains in my neck, and my wife was suffering from her replaced hips. I dropped a heavy rod on her bare ankle. The central legs refused to touch the ground. The canvas roof had shrunk. Trying to force it, I tore the anti-mosquito netting of the window. Two scorpions emerged from the folds and scuttled over my sandals causing me to drop the frame. A metal end gouged a hole on my sunburnt balding patch, attracting a cluster of horse-flies. My wife saw the scorpions and dropped the other rod on my ankle.

It was an hour before, bleeding and battered, we had got the outer canvas roughly in place. My wife surveyed it realistically.

'We'd better take it down.'

I made an unprintable reply. We broke for a beer.

'Leave it to me,' said I, in the words of many a foolish British male. I could not face taking it down. For another half-hour I struggled inside the stuffy, stifling tent, breaking clips, snapping strained rubber rings, improvising with pieces of string, pursued by insects, and almost putting my hand on another scorpion. Finally I went round in the blazing sun battering bent tent pegs into what seemed to be solid rock. It was, more or less, up.

It's finished,' I said, 'and so am I'. My wife's only comment was: 'The first Mistral will blow it away.'

'I couldn't care less!'

It's still standing, though more rubber rings have snapped. No one could sleep in it, but it can stand as a memorial to our folly until the Mistral forces us to dismantle the remains. Perhaps a bivvy would be simpler next time.

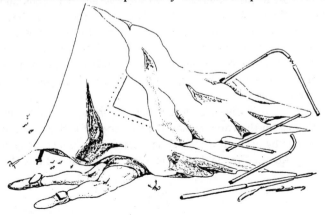

Don't let's be Beastly to the French

They lecture us about not being wholly European, they flout European rules which we keep, they call us an American dependency, pay lip service to Free Trade, burn our lamb, sabotage our fish, mock our bizarre sex scandals, and cruelly insult our national skating heroes. Hard to bear when you've only got two medals.

They have replaced us as the world's most conceited nation. First it was Britain, then Germany and the United States, then Russia and Japan. Especially since De Gaulle, the French think they are the centre of European civilisation. They claim all the important inventions, all the most important books, the greatest art, the best food and style. They even believe in the superiority of their composers. The names of British, American or German inventors are either missing from their reference books, or their inventions are attributed to the work of earlier Frenchmen.

Constable is described as 'a representative of the English cow and ditchwater school'. French history is selective. Henry I, François I, Jeanne d'Arc, Louis XIV, the Revolution, Napoleon and De Gaulle are thoroughly studied, but not the failures. What happened outside France's borders is little known, understood or cared about. Any notion that they might admit some debt of gratitude to Britain or the U.S.A. is hopelessly naïve.

In short, they behave much as we did, before our media gave us a national inferiority complex. Now that recession has shaken their confidence, they are extremely sensitive to any criticism. The French press is not interested in the sex life of its politicians. It dwells lovingly on French successes and makes light of their failures. Satire does not extend to matters of national pride.

Things look very different when you're in France. The voices at which we take offence are not the voices of a whole nation. Paris is not Provence or Gascony, and ranks somewhere below Belgium, Brittany and Germany in the estimation of most of the provinces. Most are tolerant, courteous and kind to the Britons who live among them, when they have proved that they have not come to rob or to exploit them. They even reluctantly put up with the crass behaviour of British lager louts and the rudeness of English tourists, who shout at them and always seem to think-without any justification-that they are being, have been or are about to be cheated. They know that such people are not our chosen representatives.

A group of English school children were boarding a train from Paris to Calais. Most seats in the carriage had been reserved for them, and they were being shepherded by an untidy English teacher. Many French hosts had come to say goodbye. An old French lady had reserved a seat next to the English children. The teacher told her in painfully bad French that she had no right to be there; he had asked for all the kids to be together, and she must leave. She pointed to her reservation; he raised his voice and swore at her. Finally the ticket collector came and said she was right. The teacher, however, went on making such a fuss that the old lady said she would go rather than prolong an unpleasant scene. The teacher then turned to his embarrassed flock and said, in full hearing of the French hosts: 'Let that be a lesson to you in the way to deal with these people. Never give way, firmness is the only language they understand.'

Everyone cringed. Incidents like that are not rare. No wonder a dim view of us has become widespread.

During many years in France my wife and I have received outstanding help and hospitality, apart from the superb care of their generally much superior medical services, with more G.P.s and specialists per 100,000, no waiting lists, infinite courtesy and unbelievably low charges, 70% of which are recoverable.

Revisiting after 13 years an area where I had several times played rugby with Scottish teams, my wife and I were recognised in the local bistro by the ex-fly-half barman. Drinks were on the house; he handed over the bar and brought us to the former captain, now mayor, who invited the remaining members of the team. His wife promptly laid on a superb meal for all of us. He produced a film of the match and a recording of the speeches. We stayed up reminiscing until 3 a.m.

On another occasion our tent collapsed in a huge storm. The car was bogged down; we had spent a soaked and miserable night and were covered in mud. A passing motorist stopped, tried to get our car out, failed, took us home, dried us, fed us, warmed us and, when the sun came out, returned us, helping us to tidy up and, this time, extracted our car successfully. He refused to allow us even to pay for the petrol.

Our neighbours are a great nation. They have weaknesses, but the most serious of these is that they are too like what we were in the days when we mattered. The fact that we have both come down in the world (we more than they) has made us over-sensitive to criticism - and insular. But in respect of hospitality and friendship to strangers in our midst, we are not in the same class.

Heaven-scented Lavender

The Germans have an expression 'Er lebt win der liebe Gott in Frankreich'. Literally it means: 'He's living like dear God in France', but it is often loosely used for 'leading the life of Reilly'

How right the Germans are. Morning after morning my wife and I roll out of bed into warm sunshine, breakfasting on coffee and baguettes, sitting in deck chairs listening to Mozart and Schubert, gazing in wonder at mile after mile of glorious countryside: olive groves and vineyards, great rocky mountains, maquis, pinède, chênaie and garrigue. In May the hills are thick with broom; the yellow blossom gives off a heavy perfume which gives us cheerful dreams of heroism and popularity. The little cabanon is surrounded by geraniums and oleanders, thyme, rosemary and, especially, lavender. Nature is marvellous throughout the year; light and colour change every month and every hour of the day. Olive trees are grey, or blue, or dusted with yellow flowers; they dance and shimmer, turned to silver in the mistral. In autumn the valleys are filled with cotton wool mist, and the peaks are pink and gold. Tree frogs and nightingales bring music to dusk, contrasting like Satchmo and Bing, and the quiet of night purrs with the reeling of nightjars punctuated by the ringing calls of tiny scops owls. Flocks of bee eaters flash and wheel an hour before sunset, golden orioles black and gorse-yellow flute away at dawn, hoopoes flop like gaudy butterflies on the path, and at midday the short-toed eagle gives a masterly display of flying. It hovers in high winds with no more than a lazy adjustment of a pinion here or there, it glides on motionless wings at an astonishing speed, it swoops down on snakes with half closed wings from 1,000 feet or spirals effortlessly up on thermals, until the sparrowhawks which mob it are left far behind, and even our binoculars can follow them no more.

Most lovely of all are the butterflies, which transform the big clump of lavender beside the desk where I am writing into a riot of living colour. From May to September, some of Europe's most spectacular and exotic species jostle for a place. Yellow is provided by Cleopatra, a lemon-yellow and orange butterfly of exquisite underwing tracery, three kinds of swallowtails, and clouded yellows. The dark chocolate and orange two-tailed pasha with its swift headlong flight, the hummingbird hawk moths, the painted ladies, the southern white admirals,the dark green and red spotted burnets, the brilliant tiger moths, the rich chestnut fritillaries and the delicate blues and coppers give way at evening to all the big and beautiful hawk moths.

fritillaries and the delicate blues and coppers give way at evening to all the big and beautiful hawk moths.

The smell of Provence is rich and varied: a background of pine and thyme, a foreground of rosemary and lavender. The badgers, beech martins, red squirrels and wild boar are still common. It is the ultimate place in which to live.

When the seventh day came (days are a long time in the perspective of Creation), I suppose that God did indeed sit back in a deck chair in Provence, permit Himself a smile of satisfaction, pour out a glass of Gigondas 90, (He always did prefer the good to the up-market), gaze at the clump of lavender, fill His nostrils with the perfume and say, 'Behold, it is good'.

Perhaps, however, a flash of bright red caught His eye. He may have looked more closely. For the clump of lavender is a hive of unexpected activity - murder most vile. In the most attractive blossoms, the scarlet and black assassin bug is waiting to plunge its sharp proboscis into any bee or wasp which comes near, sucking its life away until it is a dry husk. The giant hairy robber fly, bigger than a bumble bee and with golden fuzz on its legs, will eat even hornets. The praying mantis, six centimetres long, shoots out her Captain Hook forelegs and devours the fluttering swallowtails - or, if she is in the mood, the mate who has just made love to her.

Lizards and geckoes make short work of them all - assassin bugs, robber flies and mantisses - and armies of ants stand by to finish off uneaten casualties. The southern smooth snake eats the geckoes, whose all too human hands protrude from his jaws in sad farewell. The short-toed eagle above, and the badger below are waiting for the smooth snake to stray a yard too far from shelter.

A cloud of sadness passed over God's handsome face. He finished His Gigondas and rose from His deck chair. As He did so, there was the sound of shot. The eagle plummeted down from 3,000 feet, its power and its beauty turned to a shapeless sack of feathers. God's sadness changed to anger, almost despair. 'I gave man a brain and potential for a soul. I even gave him glimpses of love. From him I hoped for better......'

He sighed: 'Where did I go wrong?' He turned His mind back to the intractable problems of suffering and free will, and made His way back yet again to the Great Drawing Board in the sky.

121

A Village Remembers

Returning to England after nine weeks somewhere in France, my attention was caught by the headline, 'Butcher of Lyons to be extradited'. It was accompanied by a photo of a well-groomed middle-aged man, of harmless civil service appearance: Klaus Altmann, alias Barbie.

There was a brief report to the effect that repeated representations from the French authorities had at last persuaded Bolivia, where he had been making a successful career, to hand him over. He faced charges of being responsible for torturing and killing Resistance fighters and women and children from the south and south-east of France. Since then he has become news.

My mind went back at once to the village square at X last August. X is a little village which has been under Communist management ever since the war. Not that the local brand of Communism has much in common with the British variety - or the Soviet for that matter.

Most of the Party in X are home and property owners, who would be furious at any suggestion that a man's wealth should not be passed on to his family. For these people, to be Communist means to be anti-Boche. In X the memory of the Resistance is as strong as anywhere in Europe, for it is a village where the older generation dominates, and it is a village with a story. The story is kept alive by the group of villagers who, as many of them are reaching or have reached retiring age, meet increasingly often for a pastis and a game of pétanque at the 'Cercle de la Fraternité'.

The story is a long one, a theme with variations, for it covers adventure, heroism and betrayal over the whole period of the occupation. It was some 38 years ago, but although time may have brought some embellishments to the variations, the truth of the main theme is constant, and memories are surprisingly clear.

Position in the village hierarchy is still largely determined by the record of those days. Peacetime may have brought beer bellies and benign smiles to these veterans, but they are as tough as old farm leather and still have the ability to look, on occasions, like recently retired hitmen of the Mafia. The old gibe that there were 6,000 members of the Resistance before peace was signed, and some hundreds of thousands the day after, was not true in this corner of France. Bullet holes are still visible, perhaps still preserved, on the wall of the church, against which, on August 15th, 1944, six villagers in their late teens or early 20s were shot by Germans acting under the authority of the 'Butcher of Lyons'. The war was in its final stages, the Anglo-American armies were streaming across the northern plains and advancing from the south. The young men had been prematurely and rashly brave, and a Frenchman in authority in the village had betrayed them.

On August 15th, 1982, seeing a crowd in the village square, I stopped my car and got out to listen. There were flags by the plaque commemorating the death of the young men, and the Mayor was speaking. I had once approached him on an earlier visit to ask a favour. Erect and watchful, though wrinkled, frail and some 80 years old, he had said nothing for a few seconds. I wondered whether he had heard my question. Then he asked me whether I had fought against the Germans. When I said yes, he nodded briefly and granted my request. He had been in office without interruption since 1944, and, although he was normally monosyllabic, he had a natural dignity and confidence which, on this later and official occasion, was allied to unexpected eloquence as he warmed to his subject and introduced a larger and younger speaker who must have been an ex-Resistance hero from the Prefecture.

The theme of the speeches was simple and strongly applauded. They did not want to keep hatred alive, and they did not seek revenge. The younger generation no longer knew the truth and the historians were more and more blurring the facts. If present judgments were not based on a just and accurate knowledge of the past, they were unreliable. When the generation of the Resistance had gone, the truth must not go with them...and so they would be glad to know that the Butcher of Lyons, whom they knew to be responsible for the death of some 600 French women and children, might at last be extradited and brought to trial.

The little crowd dispersed. The really interesting part of the story, however, was not retold on that occasion. The Mayor himself certainly never refers to it. It seems that the senior French official who had betrayed the young men was himself swiftly and efficiently bumped off at a later convenient time. The present Mayor has enjoyed the confidence and respect of his village ever since.

If I were Klaus Altmann, alias Barbie, I would not rely too strongly on the possibility that memories in the Midi will prove short.

Symphonie Pastorale

Village life in England is not what it was. The supermarket drives out the little shop, the social divisions of the big towns spread like an infectious disease, the vulgar modern sameness of buildings, of juke box culture and television education destroys both individuality and the community spirit.

France has done better. True, the big towns, the suburbs and the tourist areas have been submerged in the international garishness of chromium and bad pop music as quickly as anywhere. But France is a big country. The farmers and villagers are still the most important part of the nation, still rejoicing in their independence and individuality, hard working and hard playing. Among many delightful villages, none is more charming than my 'find'.

A few tourists have discovered this place., but it is far enough from the Mediterranean resorts to attract only such people as are happy to be absorbed in the village life themselves. It has marvellous views and an ideal climate. It is an area proud of its Maquis associations and left wing loyalty, although it is itself considered a comparatively bourgeois community. It has a population of less than 3,000, although it is a market and local capital for olive and grape growers. It is largely self-sufficient in terms of builders, mechanics, doctors-or anyone you care to mention who is needed to do anything important for anyone else. Perhaps because they work so hard at other times, the villagers seem to have the leisure to be in one of the three or four large village squares from noon until 2.30 and from 6.30 to 11 at night-or long after if it should be a feast day, of which there is no shortage.

One square in the centre of the village is covered with tables from the rival cafés and restaurants, leaving barely enough space for the traffic to thread its way through. Another square is meant to be a car park, but is in practice mainly reserved for earnest players of pétanque. A third acts as a centre for fairs, dances, the circus or concerts-all are sheltered from the burning sun by a superb canopy of plane trees, and each has a fountain of ice-cold, pure spring drinking water. The village lives in its streets and squares; top priority is talk, not drinking. In the quiet and narrow back streets that wind their way up and down the hillside, old ladies in black sit on benches or on their doorsteps gathering the gossip and ruling the roost until they drop. Everyone knows everyone else and their business. The children play in the streets until their parents are ready to go to bed. There is always something doing or about to be doing, or time to talk.

In the winter, the wild boar hunts are as successful as ever and provide the menfolk with rip-roaring social occasions. In between times there is always the *chasse aux grives,* when the wretched fieldfares are eaten as soon as the migration starts, or made into excellent thrush pâté. It is, however, a caring place. The nuns are very active and, because the southern sun and the mountain air make such an excellent combination, there are old people's homes and children's sanitoria for those with chest troubles.

Although the *gendarmes* have (against great opposition) had a new regional headquarters built near the church, they do not interfere with life more than is wise in a rural area where family feuds and village affairs sort themselves out in more traditional ways. The church itself is no more full than modern churches are liable to be; the repair funds need more support, and there is plenty of good, old-fashioned French anti-clericalism, but the Catholic influence is still felt in the strength of family life and the absence of decadence as we know it.

The château has been bought by an enterprising English widow who has been adopted by the village. She is very much at the centre of life, together with a retired lawyer, the manager of the *Commerce,* and his wife. On the last night of our stay the 'happening' was the visit of our area symphony orchestra, on a mission to popularise classical music, subsidised by the regional capital. There was a full house. It was neither better nor worse than a rural orchestra in the remote parts of England, but the open air setting was remarkable. Those villagers who were not attending continued their games of pétanque or their evening pastis. As darkness gathered, coloured lights in the plane trees created a gay mood of expectancy, and when the floodlighting was turned on to the stage there came melodramatic Latin gasps of delight. A local artist had done a backcloth portraying the spectacular local landscape, where golden eagles can be seen from the main road. A good-looking conductor in white tie sprang to the rostrum and drew enthusiastic applause.

For an Englishman it was a bizarre evening. The *Suite L'Arlésienne, La Pie Voleuse,* light modern French classics, four saxophone players of high quality rendering four-part Scarlatti pieces extraordinarily effectively. There was no contaminating breath from Germanic composers. One of the French horn players was unashamedly drunk and hugely delighted with his catastrophic contributions, a delight not shared by his stony-faced neighbour. The same kind of people that prop up English orchestras were clearly recognisable: the white-haired old lady in the second violins, whom no one had the heart to drop after the orchestra had begun to take itself seriously; the boy prodigy, who was a really promising flute player, but was racked with nerves in the solos; the lady cellist assiduously cultivating a resemblance to Mme Suggia, which was unfortunately only physical; a retired schoolmaster and a bank clerk on each side of the highly competent professional oboe player; and the balding and bespectacled gentleman who revelled in his dramatic effects on the timpani and who beamed at all the ladies after each flourish.

Most of the audience, which spanned all ages, listened with apparent deep emotional involvement, taking the rough with the smooth. Others, including a whole row of unsupervised and undisciplined children who rushed hither and thither, did not. A large, friendly brown dog escaped twice and ran about amongst the players wagging its tail and licking the bow hand of a small first violin, finally relieving itself against a bass's music stand. No one cared. A local press photographer prowled on bended knees like Groucho Marx amongst the players, suddenly rising at the most sentimental of pianissimos to take flash close-ups of the young flautist or the most handsome of the saxophones. Sometimes the applause came at the right moment, sometimes not. No one left at the interval. It was 11 o'clock before it was all over and the audience drifted back towards the *Commerce*. The animation, good looks and friendliness of that audience of three hundred, consisting almost entirely of the villagers, was quite remarkable.

Two nights before it had been a *jour de fête* with all night dancing: the next night a highly unsophisticated circus. A quotation flashed into my mind: 'Dost thou think because thou art virtuous there shall be no more cakes and ale?' If only the British had not lost the capacity to enjoy themselves because of their virtuousness, it might not be so sad. There is no vice about the zest and fun at this village. No cakes and ale perhaps, but certainly olives and pastis. Their song and dance is not tourist fodder, nor high living for the rich-just part of village life, for which Britons have got too tired, divided or worried. Thank goodness there are still some corners of Merrie France to provide a reminder for Sadde Olde England.

Old Age

The Sky is Still Blue

'What's it like being over 60, Grandpa?' An unguarded expression of morning gloom on my face must have caught my grandson's attention. He momentarily abandoned the construction of his complex Lego space ship and transfixed me with a bright truth-demanding eye. I peered nervously down at him over half glasses: he wanted an answer.

Ye gods! What was there to say? It was April, but wild March winds were rattling the windows, and the grey skies were giving way to bleak hail clouds. In the last few years I had watched father and mother, father-in-law and mother-in-law die. Brother had had a stroke and his wife a coronary with three by-passes inserted. My wife had just had a major operation. One of the younger generation had died abruptly, unexpectedly and tragically. At an age when presidents and prime ministers had 20 years at the top to look forward to I was pottering around, on the shelf, getting the coal and doing the hoovering, while his mummy and daddy, aunts and uncles, as is the wont of their generation, stayed in bed until the world was safe from housework.

My Self looked out through the windows of the degenerating body which was its prison at my grandson's suddenly anxious Self peeping out of his bouncing energetic body. The extraordinary thing is that my Self is so little changed-still anxious and uncertain, still full of unrealistic dreams for the future. Curiously enough death fills my thoughts less with the passing years. There is little more shattering than losing a beloved puppy with which you grew up, as your first experience of death at the age of seven or eight.

What reassurance could I possibly offer the little man? I could tell him truthfully that my imprisoned Self feels exactly the same as his - it still likes sunshine and music and ice cream, even if it likes pork crackling, oysters and roast beef more. It thrives on wine as he thrives on chocolate - even if there is a problem over supplying ever-higher octane fuel from an ever-decreasing income. It still feels a quickening of the pulse at the sight of a rising trout and dreams unreasonably of high-speed skiing, in spite of the 16 stone deposited round it by the luxuries welcomed by its miraculously preserved tum. The sky is still blue, and water splashing and delightful. One can still love, and laugh.

This is probably the moment for an attempt at serious grandfatherly advice. I should be telling him the answers to the great problems: why we are here, peering at each other, where we are going and what it's all about. Why he need not be frightened of death, disease and poverty.

The springtime hailstorm chose that moment to stop and the sun shone through. The small boy smiled impatiently at my hesitation, but still waited for an answer. I remembered the fun of writing, that I would be returning to France next summer and that I was conscious of no pain, no imminent disasters, no immediate fear. That is sufficient cause for happiness in a marvellous if puzzling world. Age has unexpected compensations. To be out of the rat race, the competition and the need to pretend is a marvellous relief. There is time to enjoy the things which you stupidly set aside when you were competing: looking at people and at nature, sketching, writing, fishing, above all living through one's family - no longer giving a damn what people think.

Incredibly, the battle of life is still fun and worthwhile; and being a grand-father is one of the main reasons for it. Family seems to bring more joys as one gets older.

'It's pretty good, really, ' I answered. 'You'd be surprised. Finish your Lego: it's nearly story time. Ask your dad to get me a gin and Dubonnet...with ice!' complex when I go into any food shop.

The Pitfalls of this Shopping Business....

When we retire, some of us abruptly realise how much our wives have shielded us from - among other things - the necessity of learning how to shop.

Oh, I know that we males periodically buy things - a car, a squash racket, fishing tackle or shoes and clothes. No one else's tum can be measured for you, and there are one or two spheres left in which you know your own mind. But daily shopping is different. I am still overwhelmed by a massive inferioritycomplex when I go into any food shop.

complex when I go into any food shop.

Experienced housewives have no idea how dauntingly efficient they are. They know exactly what they want, they decisively reject what is substandard or overpriced, they sniff melons and prod avocados, they never fiddle about looking for cash, they pack everything neatly and speedily without overspill, and are gone before you have even found your shopping list.

Shopkeepers in Holt are very kind. They know a fool when they see one, smile amiably (if pityingly) and resist the temptation to raise an eyebrow as you hold up the queue yet again. In spite of their tactful prompting, I can't get it right.

That shopping list I eventually pull out of the basket turns out to be yesterday's, so I have to rely on my leaking memory. As I drop the five-pound bag of spuds into the basket, I suddenly realise that it must have landed on the soft creamy tea cakes I have just bought. I soon fill my first basket, so, while I push the other one forward, I deposit the first on the floor. It topples over, disgorging a cascade of tomatoes, apples and prawns all over the shop. On bending down to pick them up, I bump heads with the assistant, almost knocking her out. At this stage I wonder whether the leeks I've just bought are past their best, but haven't the heart or the confidence to hold anyone up yet again while I return them.

Time to pay. Have you any idea how many pockets a male in a winter anorak has got? Three in the anorak, four in the blazer beneath and three in the trousers. Blast! I must have transferred the money from my wallet to make it more quickly available, and now I've forgotten where I put it. By now other customers in the queue are beginning to shuffle their feet. The looks are less kindly and pitying. At last I locate the money, all small change, after a deal of patting and unzipping, in the tenth and last pocket. When I try to do up the anorak the zip gets stuck. The cash unfortunately proves to be not enough - by fifty pence.

'It's all right, Mr Lockhart, you can drop it in next time!' I am too embarrassed to do this, so I put my baskets in the corner and rush to the bank. No cheque book, of course, but they oblige with the necessary. Funny! I'm sure I took enough money. I go through my pockets again. This time I find three fivers.

In the end I settle up and go home. My wife greets me more in hope than expectation and I produce the two baskets full with a proud flourish. No potatoes. I'd left them on the floor of the shop when I had removed them from the top of the obviously squashed cream cakes.

Shopping for presents is no easier. I am paralysed by sheer financial terror.

Some people like writing out cheques, but I find it agonising - something to do with my Scottish ancestry, I fear. It's been an expensive time - four new grandchildren in as many years - so we make the usual agreements. A no present pact between the oldies and a strict limit on amounts spent on each other for the younger generation. I might have known! It never works. Foolishly generous grown-up children always cheat, sabotaging the venture with costly presents to their parents. It is understandable. You may go into the shop honorably determined to spend no more than, shall we say, ten pounds per grandchild. You know, of course, that a tenner now only buys five pounds worth of goods, but this year it soon becomes clear that it will only buy one pound's worth.

It is ten years since I decided to buy a ping pong set for my teenage son. I started with a ping pong bat (or was it a table tennis racket?), choosing a well-sponged model for £4.50. I offered the shop assistant a fiver.

'I think there's some mistake, Sir! Forty-five pounds, please!' As this was ten years ago, I assume that it would now cost at least a couple of hundred.... I gave up the attempt to buy our way into the table tennis millionaire's club.

Never mind, perhaps all will be well this year. But a preliminary look has not been encouraging. In the very unlikely event of my parting with £100 for a teddy bear, I should at least hope that it would not be cross-eyed and sullen. It would be more creative to buy my musical grandson a clarinet. For £350.....?

Getting on with Good Living - and Dying

The trouble with a grown-up family is that they tell you home truths. When you mislay your specs, again, forget an old friend's name, lose your pen and can't find your second list of things to remember to do today, they no longer smile at your professorial absentmindedness. They just tell you that you're senile, and that it's time you were put down. To have your son hit you unexpectedly on the back of the head with a croquet mallet at that distressing moment when it has become evident that you have become a burden to yourself and to the family might be one of the most acceptable ways of dying.

Other civilisations have been sympathetic to that kind of thing. I read somewhere that it was the practice in one Eskimo tribe to hold a huge party when a senior male decides that he is too old either to go on the big winter hunt with the other males, or to give adequate satisfaction to their wives while they are away. When he is sufficiently inebriated, he hands a well-greased noose to his eldest son, who plies him with the best drink until he is insensible, the same end result seem to be finding increasing support in Britain.

Seriously, senility is a sad, and in many ways, an increasing problem. In the days before everybody stopped us doing what we liked, people didn't often get senile, they just died. In the meantime many of us have to face the downsliding 60s, an increasing number enter upon the creaky 70s and quite a few are tottering on into the decrepit 80s. East Anglia has a reputation for longevity. In 50 years' time most of you who are now 30 or 40 will, if you behave yourselves and do as you are told, be heading for your centuries. Good luck!

The prospect of celebrating thirty extra birthdays accorded to us by the wizardry of medical science is hardly alluring. You will drink each other's health in Perrier or Malvern water and tuck in to an extra ration of specially-grown fruit and raw vegetables. No smoking, no exercise, no sex, no cream, butter, sugar, bread, or pork crackling. You will have a fair proportion of other people's organs, a plastic bag or two with tubes occasionally attached to boosting machines. Periodic visits from the tax man, the lawyer, the chaplain, two or three specialists and the chairman of the life support switching-off committee will provide you with companionship.

You have to admire the marvellous achievements of modern medicine. Indeed we should be foolish not to do so, for we must all pass through their hands in the end. We know on which side our bread is margarined. But I do not wish to score a century.

Our forefathers, if rich, stuffed themselves full of every delicious food they could afford and rushed about the country, huntin', shootin' and fishin'. In their late middle years they died in their own homes after falling off horses, after surfeits of lampreys or after being shot by their mistress's husbands. If they were poor they ate less, worked harder and survived a little longer. They also died in their own homes, because they could afford nothing else. In those pre-anaesthetic days death might in any case seemed preferable to hospital.

Most of us are cowards, perhaps more so now than then. We naturally fear the moment when we may no longer hope to be of any help to others, or to do anything better tomorrow than today, or to know anything but increasing pain and feebleness, But death may never come that way. In the meantime, if we are lucky, we may look forward to doing gentler things more gently, and to doing some of them better. We can hope to be kinder to ourselves and to others.

While we have to pay a little heed to the doctors, it may be time to have a little warmth at sunset. They frightened me out of smoking 20 years ago, but they didn't frighten me quite enough about booze, and I cannot now reconcile myself to a diet of brown rice and raw vegetables.....one day, O Lord, perhaps, but not yet I pray.

Like all readers as weak as I, I shall no doubt regret it. Refusal of doctors' advice will shorten our lives. Because they are humane and kind, the doctors

Like all readers as weak as I, I shall no doubt regret it. Refusal of doctors' advice will shorten our lives. Because they are humane and kind, the doctors will probably not say 'I told you so', they will ease our deservedly premature departure with a skill and care we shall not have merited. Yet I am not certain that my children and grandchildren will be much better off for those extra years. Perhaps our traditional three score and ten could be extended for those of us who are more robust to 80 or 90 - but 100 plus? It may be OK for those splendid natives of the Himalayan Shangri La who give birth at 55 and play polo at 110: mountain mineral water, goat's milk and apricots, pure air and no worries, I'm told. But not for me, and I hope not for you.

What matters is quality of life; you can forget the quantity.

In Praise of the Ugly and the Old

One of the nastiest things about modern times is the exclusive cult of youth and beauty. Fashionable beauty dominates the women's magazines, is the principle motivation for life in Hollywood and is the key to success in the scramble up our social and financial ladders.

There's nothing wrong with youth and beauty, except that the majority of us have neither. It is unjust that the western world should admire only the less experienced and wise part of its population. Every male is attracted to female beauty, and some (though undoubtedly less) women are attracted to male good looks; but to ignore the many more important factors is extremely childish. Did you listen, one Friday in December, to a serpent-tongued woman ridiculing Prince Charles because he was no longer sexually attractive? She heaped cruel insults and innuendos on his defenceless, balding head, imagining that she was being daring and witty. It is the commonest, cheapest and easiest form of negative character assassination. By the age of eight one ought to have risen above the stage of 'Yah! Big Ears!'

At some time in our early twenties we should discover that some of the ugliest people are not merely among the kindest and the wisest, but also among the most charming and the sexiest. The more women chase after fashion, the more they become alike. Their faces become perfect, smooth and boring, their attitudes converge and their figures adjust to the whims of the rag trade. Young men are beginning to follow suit. At least a substantial number of women have the sense to prefer men with ugly features, but with plenty of zing, ambition, money or charm.

One thing is certain. We shall all be ugly one day, if we survive; it may come as a surprise to find that the person peering out short-sightedly from behind the puffy eyes and waddling stiffly down the street is the same in nearly every way as the one that strutted in discos with arrogant confidence in his youth. So the sooner we drop our prejudices against the old and the ugly the better.

Why do women go to such extravagant lengths to slim and to eliminate their wrinkles? Wrinkles are the battle honours of life, the true indicators of character which should be flaunted with pride. Women without wrinkles offer no hint of experience, kindliness, gaiety and humour, subtlety, wisdom, strength or originality. True, there are other kinds of wrinkles born of negativity, malice, mistrust, depression or excess. If a lady spends hours eliminating her wrinkles and attempting to look 15 years younger than she is, she betrays a lack of confidence in the story her face will tell, and she is, in any case, doomed to failure. The sight of 65-year-old ex-Hollywood stars fluttering false eyelashes, flaunting artificially-inflated breasts and flashing smiles painfully through taut, repaired flesh is not calculated to inflame tender passions. Give me a genuine crinkle-faced granny any day.

As for the modern passion for Twiggies with no bosoms worth weeping on, they offer little prospect of comfort or cheer. There comes a stage in life where most of us have to choose between becoming shrivelled prunes or over-ripe tomatoes. All too often the prunes subject themselves to rigorous diets and their companions to vinegary nagging, whereas the tomatoes indulge themselves and their mates, remaining cheerful to the end, even if the end may come a little earlier..

The majority of males are neither rich, powerful nor beautiful. As Gilbert expressed it in 'Princess Ida', the female of the species is a 'radiant being with a brain far seeing, but Man, however well behaved, at best is only a monkey shaved'. The efforts of young males to revert to the peacock role is generally doomed to failure, because most of us are nearer to Quasimodo than to Valentine. Most of us have to renounce, at an early age, the notion that female hearts will flutter at the first glimpse of our manly features.

So we had better cultivate kindness instead, and seek out wrinkled women who have the courage to look the people and the age that they really are, who are charming rather than pretty, loving rather than flashy and whose goods are not all in the shop window. There is also a chance that they may be quite pleased to welcome the companionship and love of ordinary men, of uncertain age, who are neither powerful, rich or beautiful, but just might be wise, kind, loving and brave - and perhaps even sexy.

133

Wind Surfing

When my eldest son fell in love with wind surfing,
I concluded he was round the bend. I'd always thought
of it as an elegant fad for the jet set off sun-drenched
beaches, a way of killing time between lunch time
dubonnet and evening martinis. That this industrious
thirty-four year old travel man, previously a social
cricketer and an occasional tennis player, should
suddenly wish to spend every hour of spare time
pursuing this sport with ruthless ambition was
surprising. That he should, despite his Scottish
descent, devote his savings to different models
in Barbados, the Côte d'Azur and (of all places)
England, was unexpected. But that he should
return home to Norfolk in February, immediate'
get into a wet suit, take car and equipment down
to Sheringham and disappear from view in
a force 8 gale, visibility of 300 yards and
the thermometer at 35 degrees Fahrenheit,
proved to me that he must have taken final
leave of his senses. He had sent me excited
letters about the fun of mastering Caribbean
winds. This, however, I pondered, as I peered into the mist and driving rain,
stamping my feet into the squelchy grey sand to keep pneumonia at bay and
praying for his safe return, was Something Other.

He has not shaken off the disease. His wife has had no option but to share
his madness. Although she is a mere slip of a girl, she hauls up the sail and
rides the tempest with the best of them.

I should have known better than to land myself in the South of France, a few
miles from the two of them, within easy reach of the Mediterranean and of two
marvellous lakes. Water is not my element: I drink it seldom, and swim in it
under protest when the temperature is above 85 degrees: I am normally only
lured into it when in pursuit of fish. As for the sea, it just frightens me. There
came a time, however, when I ran out of excuses. Taunted, cajoled, flattered
and bullied, I was finally brought to the beach at Nice, inescapably confronted
with plank, sail and rope, and made to get on with it.

There was a very gentle breeze. I took heart. All kinds of doddery, pot-
bellied ancients, small boys and matronly females were gliding around,
casually and without strain. What could there be to fear for an ex-Rugby
international?

Well.....I soon found out.

'Weight on your toes, not on your heels!' Splash!

'Get your feet balanced on both sides of the mast, in the MIDDLE!'

'Don't try to use your strength, just lean!'

'Manoeuvre the sail round to the other side! ...Work your way gently round the mast ... put your right foot further back now.'

Splash! Splash! Splash again. For the tenth time the salt water closed over my head. As I came up, the mast hit me on the head and I caught sight of an attractive girl roaring with laughter. As I clambered back up, heaving my 16 stones on board for the eleventh time, like a superannuated blubber seal, I wished that I had given up gin for Lent. A childhood rhyme ran insistently through my sea-addled brain:

'A bear, however hard he tries,
Grows tubby without exercise.
Our Teddy Bear is short and fat;
It's hardly to be wondered at;
He gets what exercise he can
By falling off the ottoman -
But generally seems to lack
The energy to clamber back.'

When I finally managed to remain erect for 300 yards, and was naturally totally unable to tack and sail back again, I realised that no one had warned me that I should have to swim back against the wind, towing the wretched contraption behind me.

'Well done, Dad!'..... What hypocritical nonsense! If that was well done, a man who falls off a bicycle after 10 yards is in the running for the Yellow Jersey in the Tour de France.

I went back in a high wind, and fared no better. On the third occasion, however, a miracle occurred. For a moment the wind was neither too strong nor too weak, nor did it change direction. I remained momentarily erect and, to the outward eye, more or less balanced and in control. Finding myself a couple of hundred yards from the shore, and dreading yet another swim back, I tottered desperately round the mast, went about and returned, surviving one or two grotesque lurches, to whence I had come.

No great achievement, you might think. I was far from able to wind surf. But the aches and pains mysteriously vanished, and I felt a wild rush of conceit to the head, as I splashed in, this time deliberately and into shallow water. I was Toad at the wheel, the conqueror of a new element, a pioneer of the Space Age landing on a new planet. The madness became once and for all comprehensible, and I understood that this was indeed the greatest of individual sports.

135

And so it is. I shall never be any good; sixty-year-olds should not attempt to wrestle with gales miles from the shore like the younger generation. But they can feel what it's like and enjoy modest triumphs. This is no passing fad, but a great invention to rank with and perhaps surpass skiing. It has everything that an individual sport can offer: skill, timing and balance: a struggle with or against the forces of Nature, which must be respected and can still defeat the greatest: fresh air, beauty, exhilaration and a sensation of speed. Above all you are on your own, and the equipment is simple (well...once you understand it!). The yachtsman, even the small dinghy sailor, has to calculate wind and tide, but he is enclosed, he doen't feel the slightest change in every muscle of his naked body from top to toe, he doesn't pay for the slightest mistake with a ducking.

Yet you do not need great strength, or a gifted eye. If you can swim, and if you have courage and self-reliance without rashness, you can do it within your own limits. It need not cost a fortune, and the young can learn quickly.

Even in Britain, it should become a major school sport.

Hard Music

'Can't I have some hard music, Grandpa?' Quickly weary of the last movement of the 7th symphony, the eight-year-old looked up hopefully. The poor little chap had put up with Ashkenazy playing Chopin on yesterday's school run, and Pavarotti the day before: zero ratings.

'Sorry, I haven't got any. You can bring one of your cassettes tomorrow, and then we'll take turns.'

The notion that the orgiastic hammering of Beethoven's 7th was 'soft' music, while the amorous yowlings of his favourite pop star was 'hard' seemed a bizarre reversal of the facts. However.....my plan to persuade him to like classical music was clearly failing. Why do children avoid classical music as soon as they get to school? And does it matter?

Children like pop for excellent reasons. First it tends to be rhythmical and fun; these are the easiest musical qualities for young children to understand. Second, as most of them have been brought up hearing little else, they are conditioned to it. There is also the force of fashion. To like pop is an easy way in which to become popular with one's own age group.

Does it matter, then, that it so often excludes other forms of music? Making every allowance for Oldie prejudices, I think it does. There are historical reasons for Oldie prejudices. One moment boys and girls were pleasant, obedient and hard-working, listening eagerly to Mozart in teachers' sitting rooms. Then, in the sixties, in a matter of weeks, rock, the Rolling Stones and the Beatles took over their lives. The new music went hand in hand with revolt; for some years hair, dress and appearance were slovenly, expressions sullen, and zest for work at a new low. It may have been partly the fault of an older generation which had not changed with the times, but it was not surprising that the Oldies should associate pop with the drop-out and drug world. As they peered uncomprehendingly over half-glasses at the young who didn't want what they offered, many senior music teachers wondered agonisingly where they had gone wrong.

Yet the gap has begun to close. A new generation of Oldies looked back on the Beatles and realised that they had been tuneful, artistic and almost twee. Old Cliff Richard has become more Christian than some bishops, and even Mick Jagger is rumoured to be jogging and tucking up in bed at 9 p.m. with an orange juice and *Barchester Towers*. Pop began to show increasing variety and talent. Opera singers confessed to enjoying it, and pop stars secretly listened to classical music. Tunes borrowed from Schubert, Mozart and even Bach began to turn up in pop clothing. The classical concerts were not less well attended because of the giant pop festivals, and an astonishing array of talent was revealed by 'Young Musician of the Year'.

Classical music must not now be allowed to join the distinguished band of subjects jettisoned because they bring no easy and immediate pleasure.

Although some sensitive and intelligent youngsters come to classical music through pop in their 20s, they lose by not having studied it when young. The real role of music, however labelled, is to open hearts, minds and spirits to the full range of human dreams and emotions. If we confine that range to the fashions of a particular age group at a particular time, we deprive our pupils and stunt their growth. For the beauties of order, elegance, delicacy, control, religion, harmony with nature, despair, courage, love, power and glory have often been better conveyed by other people in other times. To grow to understanding and appreciation of these forms of beauty must add to the range of sensitivity and civilisation of the young in a way they can ill afford to miss.

Teachers can hardly force-feed Beethoven. But parents can choose the great music which has the most direct appeal to the young, and surround their children with it in the first few years of their lives. Then teachers will be able to build on their foundations.

The young have innate taste which is quite as good as that of their elders. Polls to find out which hymns are most popular with children reveal that they choose those by Vaughan Williams, Handel, Sibelius, Beethoven and Bach without realising who composed them. But if our grandchildren are going to be won over to 'soft' music, the battle must be fought in the first few years - even before they go to school.

Sunshine at Evening

Periodically articles are written on retirement by people who held important and responsible jobs. Most of them say how desirable it is to keep a hand on the tiller of the world after retirement; it is the breath of life to them to go on sitting behind a desk, dictating important letters to a secretary, being deeply involved, and telling everyone else what to do, in order to avoid boredom and decline.

Not for me, I fear, nor, I guess, for many others. Although I enjoyed my 27 years as a Head, I looked forward to genuine retirement with unmixed zest.

One is, of course, initially pathetically clumsy as a shopper, cook, gardener and houseworker, but it is good, on the last slopes towards the grave, to have some sphere in which one can hope for improvement. The sheer delight of not being a responsible headmaster can only be gauged when one isn't. For 5 or even 10 years of headmastering you may be able to remain an ordinary chap under your thickening layers of precept and example. After 15 or 20 years, however, your conversion becomes complete. It becomes almost impossible to stop giving advice. You are a typical booming-voiced Head, pompous and apart, as inevitably as originally-human bishops eventually become stamped and battered into the typical episcopalian mould or managing directors become patronising and officious. If you are aware of the process and are privileged, as most of us are, to have a wife whose principal role in those years is deflationary, there is a chance that you may be redeemable in retirement.

Cheer up, there is light at the end of the road. You will never have to sack anyone again. You will be able to watch teenagers walking along country hedgerows without wondering or caring whether they are going for a smoke or in search of amorous encounters. You will never again be insincerely flattered or courted by advantage-seekers, nor have to speak half truths to individuals for the supposed advantage of the majority. You will never have to punish anyone again, nor entertain those you dislike. You will no longer have to suffer rich men and women whose great wealth makes it impossible to understand the realities facing those who are over-worked and underpaid. No more snatched lunches, sweaty beefburgers, or sandwiches curling upwards at the edges as they dry out in old age. There is a world in which people eat French bread with strong coffee for breakfast, peaches at lunchtime and ratatouille with Côtes de Provence red wine as the sun sets over the Estérel, and the nightingales and tree frogs, bring peace at evening.

You will escape from the 3% of parents who wasted 60% of your time - like the lady who had a two o'clock appointment, and who by four o'clock had not drawn breath long enough to allow me even an interrupting comment. Finally she said in all seriousness: 'Of course the real trouble with Pip, Headmaster, is that he talks too much ... I can't think where he gets it from!'

You will escape from the teacher who seems to exist on every staff who makes Himalayas out of all his molehills, and from those discontented wives who think no one else has ever had difficulties like theirs and that their husbands are insufficiently pushing and appreciated.

No one is going to interrupt your dinner any more by telling you that Robinson mi has run away, to get you out of your bath to deal with the police, to ring you up at 6 a.m. to tell you that there is a corpse in the swimming bath.

Pure joy awaits you all. You will be able to go to pubs without wondering which of those at the bar are parents or former employees or pupils. You will learn to know privacy and to talk to and live with your wife, and to celebrate with your children and play with your grandchildren. You will spend time abroad, looking happily ridiculous wearing Bermuda shorts in green and vermilion, or playshirts covered with bottles and chorus girls. You will get up late in a silk dressing gown embroidered with purple dragons and revel in painting amateurish but brilliantly-coloured landscapes. You will make your own time for writing, fishing, photographing butterflies, playing the piano, or drinking wine with eccentric friends in the sun. You will do all those precious, selfish, creative things that you were never able to pursue. You may, like me, buy, for a surprisingly small sum, a primitive hut in a most beautiful place.

At breakfast you will lie back in a deck chair listening to Schubert or Mozart, talking at leisure with your wife about the novels you've both been reading. (Remember all those years with no time to read or to top up your intellectual tanks?). You will swim in turquoise water, drink together under the plane trees of the village square and plan expeditions to picnic looking down on the mist rising from the deep dramatic Gorges du Verdon, as the short-toed eagle hovers above the sun-drenched golden peaks. You will rendez-vous at sunset with delightful new friends and talk of new and unfamiliar worlds.

No doubt it is all very reprehensible. We should be propping up the local councils, raising funds for the village churches and repaying our debt to society until it is our turn to totter exhausted into an old people's home. How lucky we have been to find a job that was both enjoyable and worthwhile, and equally lucky to be able to leave it and still afford to live. It is, of course, a delight to meet old colleagues again from time to time. Many of them were and are the salt of the earth. It is fun to talk exams, rugby, cricket and squash, and to hear the latest uproarious tales *not* broadcast on Speech Day. Good, too, to catch up with the latest issues. Forty years ago it was whether we could replace three narrow A-levels with 4 or 5 modified to resemble more closely European practice. Things do not change swiftly in that small important world!

But now my hand is well and truly off the tiller of the world. There is so little time between our last day at school and the falling of the leaves. A brief lotus life can be very sweet at evening. If you can earn even a little on the side to swell your pension, and if you are understanding enough, a place in the sun need not be prohibitively expensive. My five months in Provence every year cost considerably less than my seven months in England meeting high costs for heating and winter clothes. You can enjoy the best of both worlds. For me and my wife these years since retirement have been quite simply and in all honesty the best of our lives.

Golden Evenings

Wemeet at seven o'clock at sunset on the nights of the full moon, every month from May or June to September. Every meeting is in a different place, although a particularly successful venue may be repeated another year. Each site has to fulfil our most exacting requirements; it must have a glorious view, it must be in undisturbed countryside, near, but not visible from a minor road or track. It must be beautiful, midge and mosquito free. A relatively flat area is needed, measuring at least 8 metres by 5. We need to be out of doors within 20 miles or so of all our homes, and out of sight of curious intruders.

The weather is not an issue. In four years we have not had a drop of rain, an unpleasant wind, a cancellation, or an evening when we were not comfortable in playshirts and shorts. By good fortune we have even avoided the Mistral; perhaps that wicked wind doesn't coincide with summer's full moons.

It has proved a delightful and comparatively cheap way of enabling friends to get together in idyllic surroundings. Candlelight dinner parties are fine, but they are expensive in time, money and effort. Their glamour can only be a pale echo of the unbelievable magic of the summer sunsets and moonrises of France's most charming landscapes. Only in Provence and the Var are all these conditions met, and supplemented with unexpected bonuses of all kinds.

We too dine by candlelight; but it is hardly necessary. The glow left by the crimson, unnaturally magnified by the heat haze on the horizon, as it sets over the Mediterranean beyond the jagged peaks of the Esterel, gives way to moonlight. This softens the colours of gorse and heather with a wash of silver. It also hides our wrinkles, shines on our white hair and makes us feel young again - for we are all over sixty and most of us over seventy. It is almost light enough to read. Yet the full moon calls to the werewolf buried deep within the most civilised, and stirs the pot of our converstaions in unusual directions.

There are twelve of us: six couples of mixed nationalities. We had no apostolic example in mind, although Jesus knew what he was doing when he chose that number. Twelve seemed small enough to avoid factions, big enough to ensure variety of experience. Above all everybody could talk to everybody, and it proved an ideal number for booze and banqueting arrangements.

Each couple brings two chairs, a small table, his and her crockery and cutlery and - most importantly - one course and two bottles. One couple looks after the aperitifs and titbits, one does the starters, one does the main course, one does the salad and condiments, one does bread and cheese, and one dessert. Turns are taken throughout the season. Fortunately we all share a taste for red wine.

Within five minutes of arriving, the tables are up and laid, and the aperitifs are ready. We belong to the generation which believes in punctuality, and the six couples arrive within a couple of minutes. We drink to each other and to the setting sun as the bee eaters and alpine swifts go whiffling and trilling to their nests. A scops owl sets up its repetitive, bell-like call, and a nightjar, tree frogs, nightingales and woodlarks set up our background music. Last year, in July, a short-toed eagle glided over us on silent, motionless wings, barely 50 feet above our heads.

After the first course, the Gigondas is flowing. We start to enjoy ourselves as only the old can do. We drink to the moon and to absent friends, and we get down to the proper business of the old, which is to set the world to rights, to criticise the young, to flatter each other, and to scrape away at the not quite empty sardine tin of our lives to see if there are any as yet undisclosed treasures left. We decide what should be done about Great Problems, and we rejoice in the privilege of still being alive and aglow, and not having to do anything about them.

We are of varied species. The founder members are an English business man who has lived in Africa, Australia and Switzerland, and his redoubtable and much travelled wife. He has an R.A.F. moustache and the impeccable imperturbability and courtesy of the endangered English gent; he is also an archæologist and natural historian who discovers a story in every pile of stones. His wife has bright blue eyes and a rare zest for battle gained in a career in diplomacy, politics and writing. There is a wise and charming French managing director, who once passed top in their redoubtable Civil Service exams, and his big, formidable, but shrewd and kindly Dutch wife. There is 6 foot 4 of retired English Ambassador, with a first in P.P.E., and an American wife from the Campus of Berkeley who kowtows to no man and expresses herself with fearless vigour. There is an English doctor who has practised for thirty years in Australia with his dynamic, tiny, partridge-plump Dutch wife: the most generous of people, with a crust of cynicism failing to disguise the warmest of hearts. There is a quiet, immensely practical Scot with a back-

141

ground in the Navy and then in oil, married to an unquiet, voluble Irish leprechaun of many gifts. And my wife and I.

Time passes on and we drop off our perches. The Ambassador was killed in a car crash, in which his still brave and defiant wife had two legs and most of her ribs broken. The zestful, bright blue eyed wife got cancer and died with soldierly courage. We recruited another delighful Frenchman with a sharp, English sense of humour and a big, bright, maternal, half American half French wife.

In the meantime the glow worms still glow, and the fireflies flicker.

It takes barely five minutes to clear away, pack up, embrace, make arrangements for the next and drive back. We always pass exciting beasts on the roadside: a family of wild pigs, a couple of badgers having a tug-of-war with a snake, a roe deer, a beech marten or a pair of foxes.

My brother warned me. 'You will just go to seed and die doing nothing! People in Provence think the sun makes them immortal.'

Perhaps we are not doing our duty or saving the world. But most of us tried to do so for forty years or more. Now it's time for a little gentle living before the lights go out.

What was it all about?

What was it that we were trying to achieve in the 20th century in independent schools and as parents? How much of it survived the changing times and deserves to do so in the future?

This attempted summary inevitably reflects my own views, even if it is fairly representative of the aims of most independent schools. It is clearly modified by my own experiences: the happiness of a close-knit family, the sight of Belsen and the tragic death of my 7-year-old daughter, run over by a car as she got out of the bus on the last day of school and ran across the road in her excitement over a good report. It made me a little softer and more sympathetic to suffering.

142

I was also much influenced by my wife's genius for communication. We had teenage children of our own in our home over some 20 years, with whom we discussed absolutely everything (in marked contrast to our own parents). Our reward has been that they have been loving and kind to us throughout our lives.

I hope and believe that we should try to teach our children and our pupils:

To love God in whatever way they can think of him, even if it is only the best and highest that is inside them and outside: at the least to keep their minds open and receptive to spiritual forces and issues.

To support the good in all people and in all events.

To honour their parents and their teachers - and, as teachers and parents, to be worthy of that honour.

To treat all people with equal courtesy, whether high or low, rich or poor, important or disreputable, but to preserve inner freedom.

To learn the beauty and the power of warm and unconditional love, starting with family relationships.

To learn to concentrate on work., even if it should be immediately uncongenial or boring, for the sake of the long term joy it can bring, and to learn that hard work in a good cause can be both rewarding and fun.

To value fitness and health, to enjoy exercise, games and sport and the companionship they provide, and to learn how to practise.

To bear discomfort, pain and disaster with courage and, if possible, with humour, and to be helpful and considerate when these things strike other people.

To dispel negative emotions in themselves and in others by laughter, kindness and praise.

When difficulties arise, to look first for faults in themselves and for the best in others.

To welcome new ideas and techniques and to develop creative inventivity and imagination.

To cast the net of opportunities and interests so wide that the smallest talent may find a sphere for enthusiasm and success.

To find happiness in honest service to the community, repaying with thanks their debts to society.

To choose a livelihood which will help them to try to establish in their own small circle a pool of orderliness amid the general tendency towards dissolution, and, if possible, to help with one or two of the great problems which face our local and our world environment.

To cultivate a hobby which will keep them in contact with beauty.

Finally, to distinguish between truth and falsehood and to seek to build bridges of understanding between all the warring factions of humanity, rich and poor, old and young, black and white, management and workers, religious factions and atheists, men and women, nation and nation.

Of course we have failed in such high aims as individuals and as teachers. But it is better to have aimed at the sun and the stars, even if they are unreachable.

The stern fact that there have been, here and there, child abuse, bigotry, hypocrisy and obvious failure must not obscure the fact that some stardust has been scattered and some inspiration has spread. That is life, and it has been exciting. Being human we could hardly expect unmixed virtue and success. But we had a go.

How lucky I have been! In spite of so many horrific and unjust sufferings, in which no one can avoid some small part, it is mostly an unbelievably beautiful world, as long as we can treasure it instead of setting about its destruction. We live in a country full of unsung, brave and kindly people. I have had the privilege of caring parents and a worthwhile job, which I greatly enjoyed, many rewarding enthusiasms to share, lots of love and laughter, good friends and, above all, the undeserved blessing of a close-knit, forgiving and unreasonably affectionate wife and family. Nothing, in the end, matters more.